Contents

INTERTIDAL CREATURES
KINGDOM Animalia

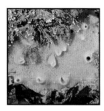

To my wonderful wife Sue,
for her love and kindness.

A PHOTOGRAPHIC GUIDE TO

Seashore Life

IN THE NORTH ATLANTIC
Canada to Cape Cod

J. Duane Sept

PRINCETON UNIVERSITY PRESS
Princeton & Oxford

Published by Princeton University Press, 41 William Street,
Princeton, New Jersey 08540

In the United Kingdom: Princeton University Press, 3 Market
Place, Woodstock, Oxfordshire OX20 1SY

Library of Congress Control Number: 2007940347

ISBN 978-0-691-13319-5

British Library Cataloging-in-Publication Data is available

The publisher would like to acknowledge the author of this
volume for providing the camera-ready copy from which this
book was printed.

Printed on acid-free paper
press.princeton.edu
Printed in Thailand
10 9 8 7 6 5 4 3 2 1

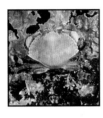

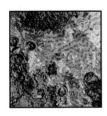

INTERTIDAL PLANTS & FUNGI
KINGDOMS Plantae & Fungi

Green Algae
PHYLUM Chlorophyta   147

Brown Algae
PHYLUM Ochrophyta   153

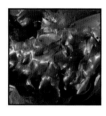

Red Algae
PHYLUM Rhodophyta   163

Flowering Plants
PHYLUM Anthophyta   173

Lichens
PHYLUM Ascomycotina   177

Introduction

The Atlantic Northeast is a harsh and wild environment with an abundance of diverse habitats for many intertidal marine life forms. Hundreds of plant and animal species live along these shores, and each of them has developed a unique niche in which it lives, coexisting with its neighbors. To learn what these species are and how they are interrelated is a step toward learning how nature works together in the giant puzzle we call life.

The intertidal zone—that part of the shoreline that is submerged in water at high tide and exposed at low tide—is a particularly gratifying place to observe both wildlife and plant life. Species are diverse, abundant, and endlessly fascinating, and many of them can be observed easily without any special knowledge or equipment. Some are animals that are found both intertidally and subtidally but whose appearance is completely transformed out of water. Sea anemones, for instance (pp. 31–34), are often seen on the beach with their tentacles retracted, and some marine worms (pp. 44–56) close their tentacles or leave distinctive signs on a beach when the tide recedes. Other species, such as painted anemone (p. 32) or Atlantic blood star (p. 131), occur in several color forms.

This guide is designed to enhance your experience of observing and identifying animal, plant, and lichen species in the many fascinating intertidal sites of the Atlantic Northeast. Many of these areas are so rugged as to seem indestructible, but in fact they are fragile ecosystems, affected by every visit from man. Please tread carefully, exercise caution (see pp. 21–22), and let your eyes, camera, and magnifying glass be your main tools for exploring the seashore.

Understanding Tides

Low and high tide from the same location.

Tides are caused primarily by the gravitational forces of both the moon and the sun upon the Earth. Although the sun is approximately 27 million times the mass of the moon, the moon is about 400 times closer to the earth, and, as a result, the moon is the dominant gravitational force that affects the earth's tidal fluctuations. In fact, the moon's gravitational force is approximately twice as strong as that of the sun.

Since the blue planet, Earth, is largely covered by oceans, the gravitational forces of both the sun and moon create a high tide, or "bulge" of water on the portions of Earth closest to the moon and sun. A similar "bulge" is also created on the opposite side of the Earth as a result of centrifugal force.

Low tides are created by a withdrawal of water from the regions around Earth that lie midway between these two "bulges." When

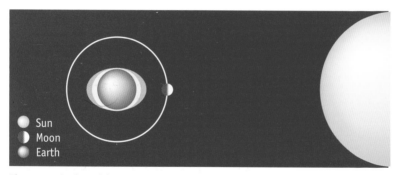

Figure 1. *Spring Tide - New Moon*.

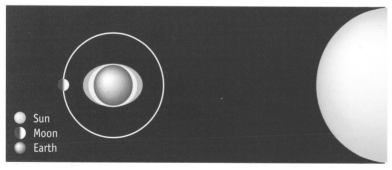

Figure 2. *Spring Tide - Full Moon*.

the "bulges" of both the moon and the sun are aligned, the highest (and lowest) tides will result (see figures 1 & 2). These are called spring tides (see figures 1 and 2), and these produce the greatest tidal fluctuations. Because these gravitational attractions are so strong together, they are said to "spring forth" onto the coast—thus they are called spring tides. (Spring tides have nothing to do with the spring season.) When these "bulges" oppose each other (at 90 degrees), they are called neap tides (see figures 3 & 4).

The Earth makes one complete revolution under the "bulge" of water during one tide cycle, so that in this area there are two high tides and two low tides during each tide cycle. Tides have the greatest range where the moon is closest to Earth. Since the moon is generally not perpendicular to the Earth's axis of rotation (the equator), the two high tides at one particular spot are usully unequal,

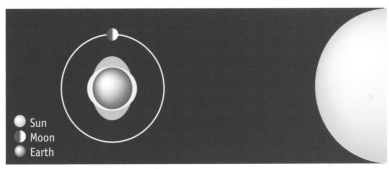

Figure 3. *Neap Tide - First Quarter.*

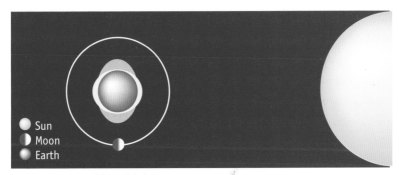

Figure 4. *Neap Tide - Third Quarter.*

one being higher than the other. The moon rotates around the Earth every 24 hours and 50 minutes. Thus the high and low tides are 50 minutes later each day. The lunar cycle is completed every 27⅓ days; thus, the moon orbits Earth 13 times each year.

On each day of the year on the Atlantic coast, there are two high tides and two lows. The best time to view intertidal creatures is close to the lowest tide, so plan to arrive an hour or two before low tide. You can find this time—as well as the predicted height of the tide—by checking tide tables, available from tourist, sporting goods, and marine supply stores and often published in local newspapers. Several excellent web-based resources provide accurate data on local tides as well. (Keep in mind that these tables are usually based on Standard Time and on a particular geographical reference point, so Daylight Savings Time and your actual location may have to be factored in.)

The highest tides in the world are found In the Atlantic Northeast, with a tidal fluctuation of approximately 53' (16 m). These tides are found in the Bay of Fundy in Nova Scotia. Here the amplitude of the tides is magnified by the funnel-shaped nature of the bay. Unfortunately, the mud shores here are not as productive for a diverse intertidal life as other habitats provide.

Tidal heights are measured from different reference points in the United States and Canada. For the most accurate information, use the reference point closest to the area you plan to visit. In the United States, tides of 0.0' are the average of the lower low tides for that year. Tides lower than this value are referred to as minus tides in the United States. In Canada, the published tide tables are 2.5' (.8 m) lower than equivalent values in the United States. Times when tide levels are lower than 0.0' in the United States and 2.5' in Canada are excellent for observing animal and plant life at intertidal sites. Any visit will be rewarding, but these are the optimum times to see intertidal life.

Understanding Intertidal Habitats

The richness of marine life found "at the edge" of the Atlantic Ocean is due in part to the wide variety of habitats in this range. Some creatures occupy a very limited habitat, hardly venturing from a small area throughout most of their adult lives, because they can tolerate a very narrow range of conditions. Other more adaptable species can be seen in several intertidal zones and into the ocean depths.

The intertidal region comprises several different habitats and zones. Each combination provides a unique set of physical conditions in which many creatures survive and coexist.

An intertidal zone is characterized by several "key" species of marine flora and fauna—species typically found within that zone. The zone may be only a favored location; the species may occur in other zones as well.

We often picture the Atlantic coast as a vast sandy beach with gentle waves rolling toward shore, but this is only one of the many environments where seashore creatures have survived for centuries.

Thousands of years have passed since the last glaciers left their enormous deposits of sand and clay. Through time, the movement of land and sea have shifted huge volumes of these materials, which have provided numerous intertidal creatures with a place to burrow. The presence of many of these animals can be detected only by a slight dimple or irregularity in the surface of the sand or mud.

Sand Beaches

Sand beaches are commonly found in both exposed and protected sites. Exposed sandy areas occur as sandspits or sand beaches. Atlantic surfclam (p. 99) is commonly seen on such beaches. This species is well adapted to survive the turbulent surf-pounded beach. Like most species found here, it has the ability to bury itself in the sand, which protects it from the pounding surf. Protected beaches or sand flats, away from the pounding surf, are a significantly different habitat, often occupied by common sand dollar (p. 137), sevenspine bay shrimp (p. 118), and other species that are not adapted to the pounding waves of the outer coast.

Mud Flats

Mud flats are situated in sheltered locations such as bays and estuaries. Like sandy shores, they support a smaller variety of obvious intertidal life than rocky shorelines do. Bloodworm (p. 49) and northern quahog (p. 105) are species to look for in these areas.

Several species are characteristic of both mud flats and sand beaches. These include northern moonsnail (p. 73), Atlantic jack-knife-clam (p. 102), and softshell-clam (p. 106).

Rocky Shores

Creatures have evolved special adaptations to live in certain habitats, so different species are found on exposed rocky shores than on sheltered ones. Blue mussel (p. 92) and northern rock barnacle (p. 112) occur in exposed areas, whereas more sheltered rocky sites harbor such creatures as painted anemone (p. 32) and Acadian hermit (p. 121).

To survive on exposed rocky shorelines, the inhabitants must endure a wide variety of hazards, including crashing waves and the hot sun's rays. Sea stars use their tube feet and suckers to keep their entire bodies in place, while various bivalves (clams, mussels, etc.) may use byssal threads to hold them in place. To endure the heat of the sun, some marine creatures, including sea anemones, have developed the ability to open and close. By closing and retracting their tentacles, they retain their moisture and prevent desiccation while they are out of water. Adaptations such as these ensure that intertidal creatures can survive many of the hazards that exist in this rugged environment.

Intertidal Zones

Marine biologists divide rocky shores, as all shorelines, into several distinct intertidal zones: the splash zone and the high, middle, and low intertidal zones. On rocky shores these zones are especially evident. Various creatures occur in one or more zones according to a complex combination of adaptations and environmental factors, including heat tolerance and the availability of food, shelter, and suitable substrate. The presence of predators may also limit the range of intertidal zones in which an animal or plant can live. Northern sea star (p. 130), for example, preys on blue mussels (p. 92), which pushes the mussels into a higher intertidal habitat.

Splash Zone

This zone can be easily overlooked as an intertidal zone, and the few small species present here seem to occur haphazardly. But these creatures are actually out of the water more than they are in it, so they must be quite hardy to tolerate salt, heat, and extended dry periods. The red velvet mite (p. 111) is one such species.

High Intertidal Zone

This zone is characterized by such species as rough periwinkle (p. 67), common periwinkle (p. 68), and blue mussel (p. 92). Maiden hair sea lettuce (p. 149) is one plant species that occurs in this zone, typically on the sides of rocks. (Seaweed species, like invertebrates, live in specific areas of the intertidal habitat.)

Middle Intertidal Zone

This zone, generally called the mid-intertidal zone, is home to Atlantic dogwinkle (p. 75) and painted anemone (p. 32), as well as green rope seaweed (p. 151) and northern rockweed (p. 160). Most creatures in the mid-intertidal zone are normally not found in subtidal waters.

Low Intertidal Zone

Atlantic blood star (p. 131) and green sea urchin (p. 136) are among the many creatures to be found in the low intertidal zone, site of the most diverse and abundant marine life in the entire intertidal area. Creatures here often are found in subtidal waters too. In the low intertidal zone there is more food and shelter and probably a greater chance that the animal will be caught in a very low tide, as low tides affect this zone only rarely during the year compared with the high and middle intertidal zones. The time marine life is exposed to the heat of the sun is also reduced, so heat is not a major limiting factor on the creatures of the low intertidal zone. There are also more species to be found in subtidal waters.

Micro-habitats
Several ephemeral (temporary) or small-scale habitats, often called "micro-habitats," can be good places to look for intertidal species, even when tides are high. In some cases, particular organisms are dependent upon these habitats for all or part of their lives.

Under Rocks
This environment is an important one. Whether the shore is rock, gravel, sand, or mud, many species such as daisy brittle star (p. 133), speckled flatworm (p. 44), and barnacle-eating dorid (p. 83) require this micro-habitat for survival.

Tidepools
Acadian hermit (p. 121), northern red chiton (p. 62), Atlantic rock crab (p. 123), and many other species are often found in tidepools but are not restricted to them. These creatures live in a somewhat sheltered environment that may be different from the zone in which the pool is located.

Docks, Wharves, and Pilings
These man-made sites attract a wide range of marine plants and invertebrates. Like rocky shores, they provide solid places for settling. The short plumose anemone (p. 34), blue mussel (p. 92), and red-finger aeolis (p. 87) commonly invade this habitat. Some are often attached to or living on floating docks, so viewing is not restricted to low tides, as these docks rise and fall with the tides, unlike fixed docks.

Harvesting Shellfish

One of the great pleasures of beachwalking can be gathering shellfish for a fresh dinner of seafood. Be aware that you need a license to harvest seashore life such as clams, oysters, and (in some areas) seaweeds, and there are harvesting seasons and bag limits. Before you take any shellfish, check with local officials for current restrictions. Shellfish harvest areas may also be closed due to pollution or to harmful algal blooms such as red tides (see below). Check with local authorities to make sure the area in which you wish to harvest is safe.

Red Tide

At certain times of the year, tiny algae reproduce rapidly in what is referred to as an algal bloom. Each of these algae can contain minute amounts of toxins, which are then concentrated in the body tissues of filter-feeding animals such as oysters, clams, mussels, scallops, and other shellfish. Once the bloom dies, the animals' bodies begin to cleanse themselves of the toxins naturally, a process that takes time—as little as four to six weeks, but as long as two years for species such as butter clams.

Some experts believe that harmful algal blooms can produce a poison (saxitoxin) that is 10,000 times more toxic than cyanide. So if you eat even a tiny amount of shellfish that have ingested these toxins, you can become seriously or even fatally ill with paralytic shellfish poisoning (PSP). Symptoms include difficulty in breathing, numbness of tongue and lips, tingling in fingertips and extremities, diarrhea, nausea, vomiting, abdominal pain, cramps, and chills. Reports of this ailment go as far back as human occupation along the coast.

Authorities regularly monitor shellfish for toxin levels, and affected areas are closed to shellfish harvesting. Watch for local postings of closures on public beaches and marinas, but to make sure, check with a PSP hotline or ask fisheries officials before harvesting any shellfish.

PSP (Red Tide) Hotlines

To obtain current marine toxin information, contact the following: In Canada contact the nearest Fisheries and Oceans office for the latest closures. In the United States check with the "Clam hotline" at 1-800-43-CLAMS (1-800-432-5267).

Protecting Our Marine Resources

Today more than ever it is essential for us to take responsibility for protecting our natural surroundings, including our marine environments. At many coastal sites human presence is increasing—sometimes too much so. Habitat destruction, mostly from trampling, has been severe enough to cause authorities to close some intertidal areas to the public. In most cases this is not willful damage but a result of ignorance about the fragility of seashore habitats.

To walk safely through an intertidal area, choose carefully where to step and where not to step. Sand and rock are always the best surfaces to walk on, when they are available. Mussels have strong shells that can often withstand the weight of a person without difficulty. Barnacles can also provide a secure, rough walking surface and can quickly re-colonize an area if they become dislodged. Return all rocks carefully to their original positions, taking care not to leave the underside of any rock exposed. Take all containers back with you when you leave, as well as any debris from your visit. Dogs should not accompany you on visits to intertidal sites.

Observing Intertidal Life

A magnifying glass or loupe is a must for any visit to the seashore, and a camera is the best way to take souvenirs. Another excellent item to take along is a clear plastic jar or plastic pail. Fill it with cool salt water and replace the water frequently. This will enable you to observe your finds for a short time with minimal injury to them. Make sure to return them to the exact spot where you found them. And if you must handle sea creatures, do so with damp hands so their protective slime coatings will not be harmed.

A Note of Caution

Before you visit an intertidal site, be aware of tide times and plan accordingly. During any visit to the beach it is important to stay out of low-lying areas that have no exit, and to keep a close watch on the water at all times. Many an unsuspecting beachcomber has become stranded on a temporary island formed by the incoming tide.

Strong wave action can take you by surprise. Dangerous waves are known by a number of different names—sneaker waves, rogue waves, etc.—and such powerful waves can and do take beach visitors from the shore. If you get caught off guard by a wave, the best defense is to lie flat, grabbing onto any available rocks that may provide a handhold. This will make it possible for the wave to roll over you rather than taking you out to sea. A vigorous surf can also toss logs up on shore unexpectedly. Please be careful!

Seaweeds can present a slippery obstacle to those venturing into intertidal areas. Serving as food and protection for the many creatures found along the shore, these plants cover just about everything. In some areas a two-footed and two-handed approach is necessary to move around safely. Rubber boots with a good tread will help you observe intertidal life without slipping or getting soaked. It's a good idea to exercise caution around barnacles and similar creatures, as their shells are hard and sharp-edged. Even for a short visit, take along a backpack, some drinking water, and a small first aid kit.

Visiting the intertidal sites of the Atlantic is one of the most rewarding pastimes on Earth. A little bit of preparation and a healthy dose of caution will help make every trip to the seashore a wonderful adventure.

The Scientific Classification of Living Things

All living organisms have been placed into a system of classification that was developed in the eighteenth century by Carolus Linnaeus, the father of taxonomy. This system is still being used today by scientists around the globe. This guide follows the organization of this classification system.

Organisms with similar structures are placed in the same category, and these categories are made up of sub-categories. The following hierarchy illustrates this principle:

KINGDOM – PHYLUM – class – order – family – genus – species

The organisms found at the seashore include the following groups. A representative photograph for each phylum may be found in the contents section of this guide (pp. 6–9).

ANIMALS (KINGDOM Animalia)
PHYLUM Porifera – Sponges
PHYLUM Cnidaria – Jellies, Sea Anemones, and Allies
    Class Anthozoa – Sea Anemones
    Class Hydrozoa – Hydroids and Allies
    Class Scyphozoa – True Jellies
PHYLUM Ctenophora – Comb Jellies
Marine Worms (Several PHYLA)
    PHYLUM Platyhelminthes – Flatworms
    PHYLUM Nemertea – Ribbon Worms
    PHYLUM Annelida – Segmented Worms
    PHYLUM Echiura – Echiurid Worms
PHYLUM Bryozoa – Moss Animals
PHYLUM Mollusca – Gastropods, Bivalves, and Allies
    Class Polyplacophora – Chitons
    Class Gastropoda – Limpets, Snails, and Allies
    Class Bivalvia – Clams & Allies
PHYLUM Arthropoda – Arthropods
    Class Arachnida – Arachnids
    Class Malacostraca – Shrimps, Crabs, Amphipods, and Allies
PHYLUM Echinodermata – Sea Stars, Urchins, & Sea Cucumbers
    Class Asteroidea – Sea Stars
    Class Ophiuroidea – Brittle Stars
    Class Holothuroidea – Sea Cucumbers
    Class Echinoidea – Sea Urchins and Sand Dollars
PHYLUM Chordata – Non-vertebrate Chordates
    Class Ascidiacea – Tunicates
PHYLUM Chordata – Vertebrtate Chordates
    Class Chondrichthyes - Cartilaginous Fishes
    Class Osteichthyes – Bony fishes

PLANTS (KINGDOM Plantae)
PHYLUM Chlorophyta – Green Algae
PHYLUM Ochrophyta – Brown Algae
PHYLUM Rhodophyta – Red Algae
PHYLUM Anthophyta – Flowering Plants

FUNGI (KINGDOM Fungi)
PHYLUM Ascomycotina – Lichens

Getting the Most out of This Guide

The field guide section of this book (pp. 26–180) includes color photographs of the common animals and plants to be seen along the seashore and concise information that will help you identify species. In the accounts for each species, or species group, the following information is provided:

Name

In the first line of the account, the current or most useful common English name for the species and its scientific name are given. This scientific name, by which the species is known all over the world, has two parts: the first part, which is capitalized, is the genus (a grouping of species with common characteristics), and the second part, which is not capitalized, is the species designation. For instance, the genus of painted anemone is *Urticina*; the species is *felina*. So the scientific name is *Urticina felina*. These scientific names are written in italics, while the higher classifications (kingdom, phylum, class, order, family) are capitalized but not written in italics. When subspecies are designated, a third name follows the species name (and is likewise written in italics, e.g., Ten-ridged whelk *Neptunea lyrata decemcostata*). When multiple species in one genus are treated in one account, the abbreviation for the plural of "species" (which is also "species")—spp.—is used, following the genus name. In some cases, scientific expertise is needed to determine species or even genus.

Other names

Any other common or scientific names known for the species are given.

Description
This section includes distinguishing physical features, behavior, and/or habitat information, to aid in identifying the species.

Size
This section provides dimension(s) of the largest individuals or colonies commonly seen; younger individuals are typically smaller.

Habitat
The type of area where the species lives is provided, which often helps in identification (see Understanding Intertidal Habitats, pp. 15–19).

Range
This section describes generally the area of the Atlantic where the species is found.

Notes
All accounts include this final section, which provides further information of interest, usually relating to the natural history of the species or ways in which it is used by humans for food or other purposes.

Similar species
If there are look-alike species that pose pitfalls for identification, these are treated in the relevant species account at the end (or cross-referenced).

Sponges are filter-feeding, colonial animals that live together as a larger unit. These "pore-bearing" animals are considered to be among the most primitive of organisms, because they bear no true tissues or organs. Unique to the animal world, these animals have canals throughout their body that open to the surrounding water, allowing both oxygen and food particles reach each sponge. Water (and food) enters via tiny pores called ostia. The water (and wastes) then leaves through larger pores called oscula. Spicules (lime or glass rods) make up the internal skeleton of most sponges, and these are used for their identification. There are about 5,000 species known throughout the world.

Yellow Boring Sponge *Cliona celata*

Other Names Yellow sulfur sponge, sulfur sponge, boring sponge.
Description A bright lemon yellow body protrudes from a small 0.03–0.1" (1–3 mm) hole in the shell of a variety of creatures.
Size Lobes to 0.1" (3 mm) in diameter.
Habitat On shells; low intertidal zone to depths of 400' (120 m).
Range Gulf of St. Lawrence to Gulf of Mexico.

Notes The yellow boring sponge lives on the calcareous shells of a wide variety of sea creatures, including large barnacles, some clams, moon snails, and others. This remarkable sponge bores holes in shells that are living or dead. It secretes sulfuric acid to dissolve a small portion or pit in the calcareous shell. Under favorable conditions, this sponge will overgrow its host completely.

Holes bored by the yellow boring sponge.

27

Eyed Finger Sponge *Haliclona oculata*

Other Names Finger sponge, eyed sponge; also classified as *Chaina oculata*.
Description This erect sponge is tan to grayish-brown or occasionally reddish with obvious eye-like oscula (pores). Several slender branches stem from a single base.
Size To 18" (46 cm) high, 12" (30 cm) wide.
Habitat On rocks; low intertidal zone to depths of 400' (120 m).
Range Labrador to North Carolina.

Notes Eyed finger sponge is often torn from its substrate during storms and washed ashore. The species' so-called "fingers" are often fewer and much flatter in the northern parts of its range. If you find a specimen on shore that has not been too badly worn, try viewing the large "eyes" with a hand lens.

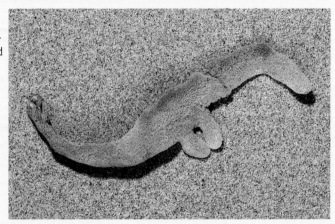

Purple Encrusting Sponge *Haliclona permollis*

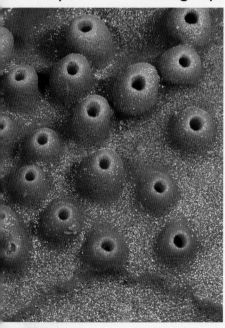

Other Names Purple sponge, violet volcano sponge, encrusting sponge.
Description The color varies from pink to purple with a soft, encrusting, or crust-like shape. Volcano-shaped oscula are found on the surface.
Size To 36" (91 cm) or more across and 1.6" (40 mm) thick
Habitat On rocks, floating docks, and in tidepools; from the low intertidal zone to subtidal water 20' (6 m) deep.
Range Gulf of St. Lawrence to Chesapeake Bay.
Notes Purple encrusting sponge is a cosmopolitan species that is both smooth and soft in texture—often with its oscula raised on tubes. This beautiful species favors sheltered waters where the water action is reduced. The classification of this sponge continues to be a subject of scientific study and discussion.

Bread Crumb Sponge *Halichondria panicea*

Other Name Crumb of bread sponge.

Description This species' color is yellow to light green overall with a soft, encrusting, or crust-like shape. Several volcano-shaped pores or oscula are found on this sponge's surface.

Size To 12" (30 cm) or more across and 2" (51 mm) thick.

Habitat On the undersides of rocks and similar hard objects as well as on wharf piles; low intertidal zone to subtidal depths of 200' (61 m).

Range Arctic to Cape Cod.

Notes This sponge gets its name from the bread crumb-like texture. If broken, it smells somewhat like gunpowder residue. This species can be found in two colors—yellow and green. The green coloration is due to the presence of green algae that live inside the sponge. At sites with rough water, the exterior of this species may have low, volcano-like oscula or excurrent pores that give the sponge a smooth appearance. In quiet waters, however, these volcano-like oscula are often prominent.

Similar Species Yellow Sun Sponge *Halichondria bowerbanki* is a yellowish sponge that has less prominent oscules with irregular spacing.

Short Plumose Anemone *Metridium senile*

SEA ANEMONES, JELLIES, AND ALLIES

Sea anemones, hydroids, and jellies (Phylum Cnidaria) (pronounced "Nye-DARE-ee-uh") all possess a central digestive system with a single opening that acts as both a mouth and anus. Tentacles with nematocysts (stinging capsules) circle this opening with radial symmetry. Each nematocyst is armed with a harpoon-like structure that may produce a toxin.

There are two stages in the life of a cnidarian—the polyp and the medusa. The polyp is the asexual stage that is often sessile (attached). The medusa is the sexual stage that is normally free-swimming.

Sea Anemones (Class Anthozoa)

Sea anemones are often thought of as "the flowers of the sea" with their colorful clusters of petal-like tentacles. In reality, the sea anemone is an animal with a column or stalk and an oral disk (disk with a mouth) capped with a ring of tentacles. Since no skeleton is present, it can flatten or extend its body by changing its internal water pressure. Reproduction may occur sexually or by simply dividing in half (cloning).

Orange-striped Anemone *Haliplanella lineata*

Other Names Striped anemone, green-striped sea anemone, lined anemone; formerly classified as *H. luciae, Diadumene lineata*.
Description The olive-green to brown body is decorated with orange, yellow, or white stripes running along the column. A total of 25–50 tentacles are present on the oral disk.
Size To 1.2" (3.5 cm) in diameter, 1.25" (3 cm) high.
Habitat On rocks, oyster shells, pilings, and vegetation, in protected areas and on mud in salt marshes; high intertidal zone to shallow depths.
Range Maine to Texas.
Notes A sharp eye is needed to spot this small anemone: its small size and general coloration makes this species easy to overlook. This colorful species feeds on drifting plankton. The orange-striped anemone primarily reproduces by splitting itself lengthwise (asexually). It is also capable of sexual reproduction.

Originating from the Western Pacific (Japan, China, and Hong Kong), this species was introduced to the Atlantic coast in approximately 1892, when it was first observed in Connecticut. Since its introduction to the Atlantic, it has permanently established itself up and down the Atlantic coastline. The orange-striped anemone has expanded its range by being transported on ships' hulls. This species has now been introduced to the Eastern Pacific, Europe, New Zealand, and Indonesia as well as the Atlantic coast.

Painted Anemone *Urticina felina*

Other Names Northern red anemone, Dahlia anemone, Christmas anemone; formerly classified as *Urticina crassicornis, Tealia felina* (occasionally misspelled *Telia felina*).

Description The colors of this species are variable and include red, purple, orange, yellow, white, or various combinations of these. Its column is smooth, with approximately 100 short, thick tentacles, often banded in white and red.

Size To 5" (12.7 cm) in diameter and 3" (7.6 cm) high, but intertidal specimens only reach half this size.

Habitat On rocks; mid-intertidal zone to depths exceeding 100' (32 m).

Range Arctic to Cape Cod.

Notes This widespread species is easily identified with its variable coloration, blunt tentacles, and lack of lines radiating from its central mouth. No sand or shell fragments accumulate on its column.

This individual is under water with tentacles retracted.

Using its many nematocysts, this colorful predator feeds on a wide variety of foods, including crabs, sea urchins, and small fish. Sea anemones attach their pedal disk (base) to a rock surface by using a combination of muscle and mucous secretions. Sea anemones are able to move along on a substrate at a very slow rate to reach a new location. The painted anemone does not produce acontia or white defensive threads. This species is also found in the Pacific Northwest and northern Europe. This anemone is known to live to 80 years.

This individual is under water with tentacles extended.

Silver-spotted Anemone *Aulactinia stella*

Other Names Gem anemone; formerly classified as *Bunodactis stella*.

Description The body is grayish-green to translucent or occasionally reddish. White lines radiate from the mouth of its oral disk, and a whitish ring is found on the 48–96 elongated tentacles. A white spot at is present at the base of each tapered tentacle, and sticky bumps are found on the column.

Size To 2" (5 cm) in diameter, 1.5" (4 cm) high.

Habitat Attached to rocks and buried in sand or sediments; low intertidal zone to shallow subtidal.

Range Nova Scotia to the Gulf of Maine.

Notes This elegant anemone usually has sand and shell fragments attached to its sticky column. This is best viewed when it is out of the water at low tide; however, it is often buried up to the edge of its disk in sand. The silver-spotted anemone broods its juveniles internally—an uncommon situation in the world of anemones. This species is preyed upon by the shag-rug nudibranch (see p. 88). In order for this predator to feed on this anemone and not become a meal itself, it secretes mucus for protection against the stinging tentacles of this anemone.

This individual is out of water with tentacles retracted.

33

Short Plumose Anemone *Metridium senile*

Other Names Frilled anemone,
plumose anemone, common sea
anemone, northern anemone, sun
anemone, white plumed anemone,
plumed anemone, powder puff
anemone, orange anemone, fluffy
anemone, white plume anemone,
sun anemone; formerly classified as
Metridium dianthus.

Description This anemone's color
may be white, yellow, orange, pink,
or brown overall. Several lobes
divide from the disk, and there may
be a total of up to 100 very thin
tentacles.

Size To 2" (5 cm) in diameter, 4"
(10 cm) high.

Habitat On rocks or similar surfaces
and wharf piles; low intertidal zone
to depths of 98' (30 m).

Range Arctic to Delaware.

This individual is under water.

Notes The short plumose anemone may be viewed from a dock by peering at the
creatures attached to the dock below the water's surface. This common species feeds
primarily on plankton, and small, free-living marine organisms, and fish. It usually
reproduces asexually: a new anemone can arise from each small piece of tissue left
behind when this species moves to a new site. As a result, a clone is formed. This
species also reproduces sexually and is capable of binary fission (dividing in half) as
well. The short plumose anemone is common along the Pacific, the Mediterranean,
and Atlantic European coasts as well as the
northern and mid-Atlantic coasts of North
America.

If disturbed, this species may discharge its
acontia—thin, white threads on its column
that contain nematocysts used as a defense
against predators. When the tentacles of
this species are retracted, as at low tide,
its shape has been compared to everything
from a bagel to a small volcano.

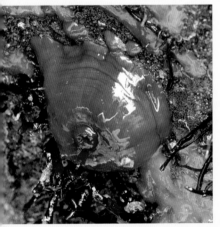

This individual is out of water.

Hydroids and Allies (Class Hydrozoa)

Most hydroids are colonial animals with a life cycle that includes both the asexual polyp (a tube-like organism) and the sexual medusa (umbrella-shaped) stage. Medusae in this class have a muscular velum or veil-like ring that helps them move through water and an exoskeleton that is made of chitin or calcium carbonate. A few hydroids resemble true jellies but are smaller in size—up to 4" (10 cm) in diameter.

Zig-zag Wine-glass Hydroid *Obelia geniculata*

Other Name Knotted thread hydroid.
Description In this species, white stalks arise from the "knee" of each stalk, giving it a zig-zag appearance. Urn-shaped sheaths around the reproductive buds have collars.
Size Polyp colony to 1" (25 mm) high, 12" (30 cm) wide.
Habitat On rocks or seaweed and in tidepools; low intertidal zone to shallow subtidal depths.
Range Arctic to Florida and Texas.
Notes The characteristic shape of zig-zag wine-glass hydroid is very distinctive. This colonial creature contains many polyps, each of which feeds on a variety of tiny organisms captured with small tentacles. The polyp is also the reproductive form that produces small buds. Each bud develops into free-swimming medusa that produces fertilized eggs, which then develop into swimming planula (larvae), the next stage in the species' life cycle. These planula eventually settle on a hard surface, where they become attached and complete their life cycle.

Wine-glass Hydroids *Campanularia* spp.

Description These species are white overall with wine-glass shaped polyps and stems that lack a zig-zag shape.
Size Polyp colony to 10" (25 cm), high 6" (15 cm) wide.
Habitat On seaweeds, rocks, pilings, or similar objects; low intertidal zone to depths of 1,380' (420 m).
Range Labrador to Florida.
Notes The life cycle of the *Campanularia* clan is different from their *Obelia* (p. 35) cousins. The medusa of wine-glass hydroids *Campanularia* spp. are not free-swimming but rather remain inside the polyps to produce the eggs, sperm, and embryos that are also not free-swimming. A microscope is necessary to observe these differences.

By-the-wind Sailor *Velella velella*

Other Names Sail jellyfish, purple sailing jellyfish; formerly classified as *V. lata*.
Description The float is a bright blue with a transparent triangular sail on the dorsal side.
Size To 2.3" (6 cm) long.
Habitat Normally on the ocean's surface but often found stranded on shore.
Range Temperate and tropical oceans worldwide.
Notes By-the-wind sailor is a floating hydroid that occasionally washes ashore by the hundreds in late spring and early summer. Its colorful base is made up of a float, which is comprised of gas-filled pockets. Its common name originates from the prominent sail that arises from the float. Although there are several tentacles that

surround this "jelly's" outer rim, they are harmless to man. This cosmopolitan species feeds on small fish eggs, cope-pods, and other marine life.

True Jellies (Class Scyphozoa)

The rhythmic pulses of jellies are intriguing to observe—indeed, their fluid movements have a near-hypnotic effect. The purpose of this movement is probably to keep the animal near the surface of the water. Its seemingly random wanderings are influenced and aided by water currents.

Jellies date back to Precambrian times: one Australian fossil has been aged at 750 million years. There are a thousand known species of these primitive carnivores, which feed primarily on zooplankton. The jelly has two distinct stages in its life cycle: it begins life as a polyp (a tube-like organism with a mouth and tentacles) and eventually transforms into a medusa (umbrella-shaped organism). A jelly captures its food and then lifts it to its mouth to eat. The medusae in the Class Scyphozoa differ from those of hydrozoans because true jellies lack a velum or veil-like ring under their bell.

Jellies are composed of as much as 96 percent water, but several species are consumed as food in various cultures where they are eaten boiled, dried, or raw.

Whitecross Hydromedusa *Staurophora mertensi*

Other Name Whitecross jellyfish.
Description The transparent flattened bell has a white cross along with many tentacles around its edge.
Size Medusa to 12" (30 cm) in diameter, 2" (51 mm) high.
Habitat Normally in the ocean but often found stranded.
Range Arctic to Rhode Island.

Notes Whitecross hydromedusa lives deeper during the daylight hours, rising near the surface at night. The bell-shaped medusa is a carnivore that dines on other medusa and crustaceans. The four radial canals have white gonads attached to them. More research on this common species is needed; little is known about its life cycle.

Atlantic Moon Jelly *Aurelia aurita*

Other Names Moon jelly, white jellyfish.

Description The translucent white dome encloses the round or horseshoe-shaped gonads (reproductive organs). Adult gonads are yellowish, brownish, pink, or purple, and immature gonads are white.

Size To 20" (50 cm) in diameter.

Habitat On or near the surface of the ocean near shore.

Range Arctic to Florida and Mexico.

Notes Atlantic moon jelly is often found washed up on the beach after a storm or merely after high tide. This species is mildly toxic; those who encounter it in the water might get a rash that itches for a few hours. The rhythmic pulsations of this species moving in the water may be easily viewed from a dock under quiet conditions. Atlantic moon jellies are carnivorous, feeding on plankton, including the larvae of mollusks, crustaceans, tunicates, and others. They have also been observed eating small jellies and comb jellies.

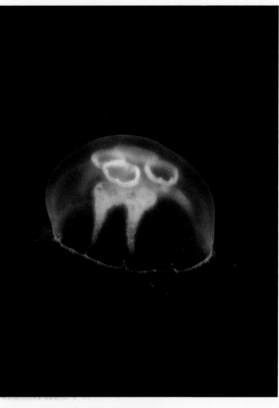

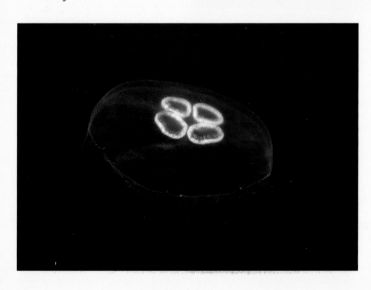

Lion's Mane *Cyanea capillata*

Other Names Lion's mane jelly, sea blubber, sea nettle, red jelly, sun jellyfish.

Description The smooth, flat-topped bell is pink, yellowish, or reddish-brown. Trailing tentacles are in 8 clusters located between the 16 lobes of the bell's margin. There are 70–150 tentacles in each cluster. Suspended beneath the bell lies a shaggy mass containing the feeding tube, lips, and ribbon-like gonads.

Size Normally to 20" (50 cm) in diameter, with tentacles to 10' (3m) long; rarely to 8' (2.5 m) in diameter and tentacles to 119' (36 m) long.

Habitat Usually found floating near the surface of the water and occasionally stranded on the beach.

Range Arctic to Florida and Mexico.

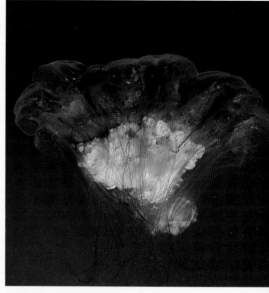

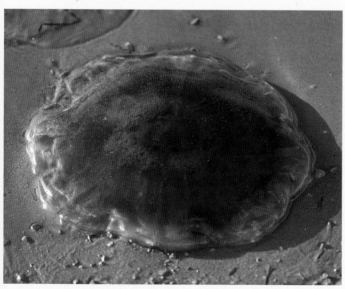

Notes Lion's mane is the largest jelly in the world. The color of this species varies greatly; older individuals are typically darker than young ones. This predator feeds on small fish, crustaceans, and other animals. Some species of fish find that the lower portion of the bell provides refuge from their enemies.

Contact with the tentacles of this toxic species produces a burning sensation. Exercise caution, even with a jelly stranded on the beach. All jellies are toxic to some degree, and human reactions vary from a mild rash to blistering and, occasionally, death. If you are stung by this species, try meat tenderizer or wet sand as an antidote.

39

Sea Grape Comb Jelly *Pleurobrachia pileus*

COMB JELLIES
Phylum Ctenophora

The transparent bodies of comb jellies resemble jellies, but they are unrelated and form a separate phylum. Numerous cilia or tiny hairs are used for locomotion by their rhythmic beating. These cilia are arranged in eight rows of ctenes or comb plates. Eggs and sperm are released into the water from the mouth where they develop into small versions of the adult. No stinging cells are present, and there is no alternation of generations as there is in the bell-shaped jellies.

Sea Grape Comb Jelly *Pleurobrachia pileus*

Other Names Sea grape, sea gooseberry, sea walnut.

Description The round to oval body is transparent and iridescent. Two fringed tentacles are present, along with 8 rows of comb plates.

Size To 1" (25 mm) wide, 1.1" (28 mm) high.

Habitat Normally found swimming near the surface of the water, often in large numbers.

Range Nova Scotia to Florida and Texas.

Notes The two long tentacles found on the sea grape comb jelly are retractable and can extend 20 times the length of the body. These tentacles bear numerous sticky cells that are used to collect food. For quite some time, it was generally believed that all comb jellies produce bioluminescence. Although light often appears to be produced by this species, researchers have determined that it and other members of the genus Pleurobrach are not capable of producing bioluminescence. The light observed on sea grape comb jellies is a product of light reflecting on the iridescent plates of the cilia. Other species, such as Beroe's common comb jelly (p. 42), however, do produce their own light at night.

Beroe's Common Comb Jelly *Beroe cucumis*

Other Names Pink slipper comb jelly, Beroid comb jelly.
Description The transparent pink or rust body often
is flattened and
sac-like. Eight rows
of comb plates are
positioned on the
outer surface.
Size To 4.5" (114
mm) long, 2" (51
mm) high.
Habitat Normally
found swimming near
the surface of the
water, often in large
numbers.
Range New
Brunswick to Cape
Cod, Massachusetts.

Individual with mouth open.

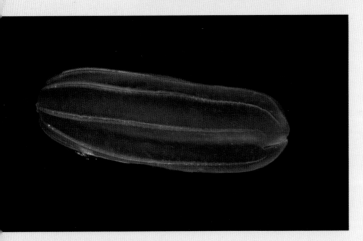

Individual with mouth closed.

Notes Beroe's common comb jelly is a predator that feeds on various medusae and
other comb jellies. This lobed comb jelly normally swims forward with its mouth
closed, opening it only to feed. Its mouth is large, taking up the entire oral end,
which helps it feed on larger prey items. Freshly caught prey can often be viewed and
identified through its transparent body wall.

Painted Fifteen-paired Scaleworm *Harmothoe imbricata*

MARINE WORMS

Phyla Platyhelminthes, Nemertea, Annelida, Echiura

M arine worms are a collection of unrelated yet similar-looking groups. These worms are classified in several phyla including flatworms, ribbon worms, segmented worms, and spoon worms.

FLATWORMS
Phylum Platyhelminthes

These unsegmented worms are characteristically flat and do not have blood or circulatory systems. Flatworms may have eyespots, light-detecting organs that are not restricted to the head region. It is estimated that there are about 25,000 living species in the world.

Speckled Flatworm *Notoplana atomata*

Description The body is grayish-brown and marked with fine flecks. No tentacles are present, and 4 clusters of ocelli or eyespots are located in the anterior portion of the body, but none are present along its margin.
Size To 1.5" (38 mm) long, .75" (19 mm) wide.
Habitat Under rocks often when the worm lies on top of gravel; low intertidal zone to deep subtidal depths.
Range New Brunswick to Cape Cod, Massachusetts.
Notes Speckled flatworm is a predator that feeds on small creatures that become

trapped in the slime it produces as it moves about. This is the most common species of flatworm found in the rocky Atlantic Northeast. It has also been found on the Pacific Coast. Other flatworm species may also be encountered, but they have tentacles, different colorations, or eyespots, in various combinations.

RIBBON WORMS
Phylum Nemertea

The worms in this group are more advanced than flatworms and have blood or circulatory systems. The ribbon worm has a retractable snout (proboscis) with either sticky glands or poisonous hooks used to capture its prey. Members of this group often fragment or constrict into several pieces when handled. Such an action is one form of asexual reproduction—each section forms a new ribbon worm.

Milky Ribbon Worm *Cerebratulus lacteus*

Other Name Milky nemertean.
Description The body is milky-white to pinkish, with a head that is grooved on the ventral side (underside).
Size To 48" (122 cm) long, .6" (16 cm) wide.
Habitat On mud and sand beaches; low intertidal zone to subtidal depths.
Range Entire Atlantic coast.
Notes Milky ribbon worm is a predator that captures its prey using its long, sticky extendable proboscis. It is a predator of concern in areas where the softshell clam (p. 106) is present, because it also preys upon larger prey, including clams. It is unclear how it actually attacks clams. One observation describes it entering the body via one of its siphons, while others believe that this ribbon worm attacks the foot first preventing the prey from withdrawing into its burrow. The ribbon worm then feeds upon the internal organs of the clam. This species normally moves about in the mud and sand, but it is also uses its flattened body to swim at night with an undulating motion. The milky ribbon worm has been reported to occasionally extend to an amazing 20' (6 m) in length.

This young individual is much shorter than an adult.

Red Lineus *Lineus ruber*

Description The color on the dorsal side is normally light to dark reddish-brown, often with a greenish-red, yellowish-brown, or violet tinge. The colors are lighter on its ventral side. There is a slit on its head and a total of 2–8 eyespots on either side of the head.

Size To 6" (150 mm) long, 0.1" (3 mm) wide.

Habitat In various muddy sites; high intertidal zone to shallow subtidal depths.
Range Maine to Long Island Sound.

Notes This common species could be easily called mud ribbon worm. Its many habitats include muddy sand under stones and rocks, among barnacles or mussels, in tidepools, in muddy estuaries, and at almost any other type of muddy site. It is also very tolerant of low salinities that reach as low as about 8%. Red lineus feeds upon various segmented worms and normally contracts when prodded. This nemertean has a circumpolar distribution in the northern hemisphere.

Similar Species Green Lineus *L. viridis* is often found at similar sites and has a wide range of colorations, including dark green to olive or bronze green or nearly black on its dorsal side, and a lighter ventral surface. Pale transverse lines are often visible along full length of its body. A slit is present on its head, as well as a row of 2–8 eyespots on each side of the head.

SEGMENTED WORMS
Phylum Annelida

All segmented worms are easily identified by the many segments that make up their bodies. Each segment contains the elements of body systems that include circulatory, nervous and excretory tracts. It is believed that segmented worms are a more advanced worm phylum since muscle contraction is localized, which allows for a more complex organism. There are three types of annelids: polychaete worms (Class Polychaeta), earthworms (Class Oligochaeta) and leeches. Most marine annelids are polychaetes (segmented worms with bristles). Over 9,000 species of segmented worms have been identified.

Polychaete Worms (Class Polychaeta)

Tufted Twelve-paired Scaleworm
Lepidonotus squamatus

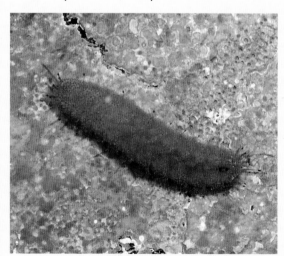

Other Names Twelve-scaled worm; scientific name also spelled as *L. squamata*.

Description The body is brown, gray, or mottled and covered with 12 pairs of scales above, with brown, green, or red projections or tufts of various sizes. The antennae and tentacles are dark-banded with pointed tips.

Size To 2" (51 mm) long, .6" (16 mm) wide.

Habitat Under rocks, on piles, on gravel, or shell debris; low intertidal zone to depths of 8000' (2438 m).

Range Labrador to New Jersey.

Notes The tufted twelve-paired scaleworm rolls up into a ball when it is threatened. This measure places its hard scales outward, thus protecting the vulnerable portions of its body. The scales of this species are not lost easily as they are in many species of scaleworms. There are other intertidal members of the twelve-paired scaleworm clan, but they live south of Cape Cod.

47

Painted Fifteen-paired Scaleworm
Harmothoe imbricata

Other Name Fifteen-scaled worm.
Description The overall color
may be black, brown, red, yellow,
speckled, mottled, or with a brown
or black dorsal stripe. The body is
covered with 15 pairs of scales on
the dorsal side and four eyes are
present below.
Size To 2.5" (65 mm) long, 0.75"
(19 mm) wide.
Habitat Under rocks, in tidepools,

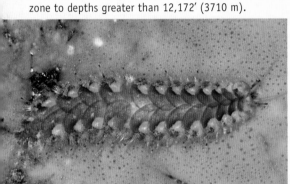

in the tubes of other worms, or in the shells occupied by hermit crabs; low intertidal
zone to depths greater than 12,172' (3710 m).

Range Arctic to New Jersey.
Notes The different
colorations of this spe-
cies are truly amazing. The
images here give some idea
of these variations. It is
also very tolerant of a wide
range of environmetal factors, including salinity and
temperature. It is occasionally found living commen-
sally or in peaceful harmony
with various tubeworms

or hermit crabs. This
species is also found
along the Pacific coast.
Females lay 5,000 to
over 40,000 eggs and
brood their eggs under
their scales in southern
California. In France,
however, the eggs are
released directly into
the ocean and are never
brooded. It is believed
that this species broods
its eggs in the North
Atlantic.

Similar Species **Four-eyed fifteen-paired scaleworm *H. extenuata*** is one of several
additional species of fifteen-paired scaleworms. This species has 4 eyes on the top of
its head.

Two-gilled Bloodworm *Glycera dibranchiata*

Other Names Bloodworm, beak thrower.

Description The pink body harbors a proboscis that displays 4 dark jaws at the tip. There is an elongated red gill above and below each parapodium or appendage.

Size To 15.4" (38 cm) long, .5" (13 mm) wide.

Habitat In mud, sand, and gravel; low intertidal zone to depths of 1,322' (403 m).

Range Gulf of St. Lawrence to West Indies.

Notes Two-gilled bloodworm appears earthworm-like when viewed out of water. It is capable of projecting its proboscis or snout an amazing distance forward. Its proboscis is used for feeding, burrowing, and defense. Using a neurotoxin, it effectively subdues its prey—amphipods and marine worms. This species is also known to "nip" the unwary. To burrow, it thrusts its proboscis into the sand as far forward as possible. The tip of the pharynx then swells and anchors itself in the sand in order to bring the animal forward. This is repeated time and time again to move forward. Eventally this creates a series of tunnels or galleries in which this bloodworm can move and feed.

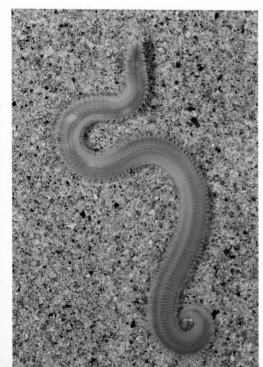

This species does not feed during the summer months of the year. During spring mature adults focus on reproduction. The sexes are separate and during the spawning season: males spawn first,followed by the females. Mature females can produce up to ten million eggs. The two-gilled bloodworm dies after spawning, leaving its empty "skeleton" on the shore.

Two-gilled bloodworm is an important food source for semipalmated sandpipers *Calidris pusilla* while on migration. It is also harvested extensively as bait for sport fishermen.

This individual is under water.

Leafy Shimmyworm *Nephtys caeca*

Other Names Leafy shimmy worm, red-lined worm.
Description The body is green, white, or bronze-colored, with leaf-like extensions behind each pair of appendages.
Size To 8" (20 cm) long, .6" (16 mm) wide.
Habitat In sand and muddy sand; mid-intertidal zone to depths of 1,312' (400 m).
Range Arctic to Rhode Island.
Notes Leafy shimmyworm is capable of regenerating various body parts that have been removed by predators. It feeds on various segmented marine (annelid) worms as it moves about through the sand. This species lives to six years and is circumpolar in its distribution.

Iridescent Sandworm *Neanthes virens*

Other Names Clamworm, ragworm; also classified as *Nereis virens*.
Description The color is iridescent greenish or bluish overall, often with gold, red, or white spots on a body that is comprised of 200 segments. There are 4 pairs of tentacles on the head, a pair of shorter tentacles on the side of mouth, and 2 lobed body appendages, each with a broad upper portion.
Size To 36" (91 cm) long, 1.75" (44 mm) wide.
Habitat In sand, mud, clay, or peat areas; high intertidal zone to depths of 500' (152 m).
Range New Brunswick to New Jersey.
Notes Male iridescent sandworms go through a remarkable transformation in order to reproduce. Males become structurally modified for swimming in order to swarm during

the new moon for fertilization of the females' eggs. After reproduction, the adults go through a mass mortality. Adults are often found dead on the beach after such swarms. A female produces between 50,000 to 1,300,000 eggs, depending upon her size. It is unclear how long adults live. Studies indicate they may live anywhere from 2 to 7 years.

This species is well known for its predatory habits on a variety of invertebrates, including other worms. It does, however, feed on carrion as well as algae. It provides an important food source for a wide variety of fish. The iridescent sandworm is commercially collected as bait for sport fishermen. **Similar Species Common sandworm *N. succinea*** is a similar species that prefers sandy mud, where it builds a U-shaped burrow. This species is greenish in color towards the anterior (front) and yellowish or reddish at the posterior (rear).

Northern Lugworm *Arenicola marina*

Other Name Lugworm.
Description The orange-brown body hosts 12 to 13 pairs of prominent red gills.
Size To 8" (20 cm) long, 0.75" (19 mm) wide.
Habitat In protected sand and muddy sand flats; low intertidal zone to shallow subtidal.
Range Arctic to Cape Cod.
Notes Northern lugworm burrows into the sand and forms an L-shaped burrow that reaches 6" (15 cm) down. Water is pumped into its burrow enabling it to irrigate its gills. Food is obtained from the sand and mud it ingests. The distinctive sand castings are then voided at the end of the burrow, leaving evidence of the worm's presence below.

Sand casting.

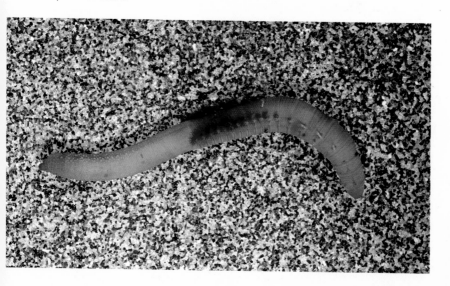

Collared Bamboo-worm *Clymenella torquata*

Other Name Bamboo worm.

Description Body is brown to light green or reddish overall with red joints. There are 17 segments; the fourth segment from the anterior end consists of a flared collar, and the last 4 segments are funnel-shaped.

Size To 6" (15 cm) long, 0.25" (6 mm) wide.

Habitat In sand and muddy sand; low intertidal zone to depths greater than 330' (100 m).

Range Bay of Fundy to North Carolina.

Tube.

Notes Bamboo-worms closely resemble their namesakes—bamboo stalks. They construct a tube from sand grains up to 10" (25 cm) long that protects them on a variety of beaches. This tube is placed upright, and they feed on sediment in the sand and mud with their head down, leaving their hind end toward the top. The top is open to predation especially by fish. It is not uncommon for up to 20% of a population to be missing their hind ends, which will eventually be regenerated.

Gould's Trumpetworm *Pectinaria gouldi*

Other Names Ice-cream-cone worm, trumpetworm; formerly classified as *Cistenides gouldi*.

Description Pink overall with red and blue markings; trumpet-shaped tube with a slight curve and 2 sets of golden bristles.

Size To 2" (5 cm) long, .25" (6 mm) wide.

Habitat Protected beaches with sandy mud; low intertidal zone to depths of 90' (27 m).

Range Bay of Fundy to Florida.

Notes The meticulous and detailed work of this small worm rivals that of the best stonemason. A close look at the remarkable tube of this species reveals an amazing precision that is hard to imagine from a worm. As the worm grows, it adds slightly larger sand grains to its tube with exacting precision. Gould's trumpetworm lives upside down inside its cone-shaped tube, feeding on microbe-coated sand grains from the sediments. Both ends are open, with the small end up and exposed for breathing.

Tube.

Potter Spaghetti-worm *Amphitrite figulus*

Other Names Johnston ornate worm, Johnston ornate terebellid; formerly classified as *Neoamphitrite figulus* and *Amphitrite johnstoni*.

Description The body is orange, pink, red, or brown overall with many long, slender, yellowish-orange tentacles extending from the head. There are a total of 23–45 segments, with 3 pairs of red gills and an abdomen that is narrower than the thorax.

Size To 10" (25 cm) long, .5" (13 mm) wide.

Habitat Under rocks; low intertidal zone to shallow depths.

Range Arctic to New Jersey.

Notes This beautiful worm builds a tube that it attaches to the bottom of a rock. Its common name comes from *figulus*, which means "potter," a reference to its pottery-like tube. From the front of its tube it extends it's many spaghetti-like tentacles to sweep the surface for minute particles of food that it transports to its mouth via cilia (hair-like projections) on grooves located on each tentacle. The sight of these tentacles on the ocean floor is often the only indication that this species (or any other spaghetti-worm) is present.

Similar Species Ornate spaghetti-worm *Amphitrite ornate* may also be encountered from Maine to North Carolina. This species reaches 15" (38 cm) long and it builds its tube underground to a depth of 12" (30 cm) or more.

Common Broom Worm *Pherusa affinis*

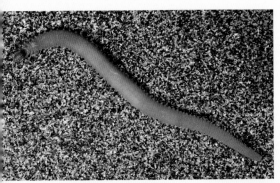

Other Names Bristleworm; also classified as *Trophonia affinis*.

Description The body is yellowish-brown with prominent bristle-like palps at the anterior end.

Size To 2.3" (58 mm) long.

Habitat In silt, sand, and mud; low intertidal zone to shallow subtidal.

Range Nova Scotia to Cape Hatteras.

Notes Common broom worm, like many other marine worms, secretes mucous that adheres to the surrounding sand, forming a tube for it to inhabit. This species is very tolerant of sludge and organic debris. The predators of this deposit feeder include crabs and fishes.

Sinistral Spiral Tubeworm *Spirorbis spirorbis*

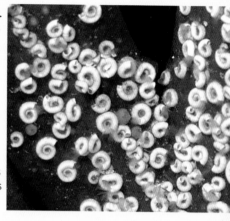

Other Name Also classified as *S. borealis*.
Description The white calcareous shell is coiled counterclockwise.
Size Coil to 0.1" (3 mm) across.
Habitat On rocks, algae, and shells; low intertidal zone to shallow subtidal.
Range Maine to Cape Cod.
Notes Sinistral spiral tubeworm is commonly encountered in the intertidal region. When the water recedes, the worm closes the opening to its shell with an operculum or trap door. This operculum is actually a modified tentacle that prevents the worm from drying out when it is not submerged. This species is hermaphroditic, with the segments toward the front being female and those at the rear male. It is also found along the entire Pacific coastline.
Similar Species Dextral spiral tubeworm *Circeis spirillum* may also be found living in this area. Its shell is coiled in a clockwise direction.

Marine Earthworms (Class Oligochaeta)

Sludge Worms *Clitellio* spp. and others

Description The pink to reddish segmented body is very slender, lacks appendages, and may appear somewhat translucent.
Size To 2.5" (63 mm) long.
Habitat In protected areas with muddy sand; high intertidal zone to subtidal depths.
Range Arctic to Florida.
Notes Sludge worms are marine earthworms (Class Oligochaeta), related to the common earthworm. Like earthworms, they do not possess anterior appendages or parapodia (extensions) on the sides of their smooth body. They are generally reddish in color due to the presence of hemoglobin. Individual species in this group are notoriously difficult to identify. Some species reach high population levels and likely provide an important food source for various birds on migration.

ECHIURAN WORMS
(Phylum Echiura, also known as Echiurida or Echiuroidea)

The echiuran worms or spoonworms are a small group of worms that are closely related to segmented worms, but spoonworms' bodies lack segments. These worms have a large non-retractable proboscis (snout) that is often grooved and spoon-shaped—the reason for their common name. The proboscis also contains the brain. Echiura means "spiny tail" in Greek, a reference to the ring or rings of bristles that encircle the end of the worm.

Spoonworms *Thalassema* spp. and others

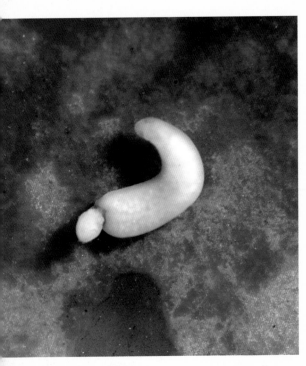

Description The color of the sausage-shaped body is pinkish. The proboscis is separate from the body.
Size To 10" (25 cm) long.
Habitat In mud and sand; low intertidal zone to subtidal depths.
Range Along the entire coast.
Notes Spoonworms are particulate feeders that secrete mucous to their capture food. The distinctive members of this phylum locomote by alternating constrictions with dilations of the body, creating rhythmic pulsations that extend the length of their body. Most spoonworms build a burrow in which they live.

Leafy Bryozoan *Flustra foliacea*

MOSS ANIMALS

Phylum Bryozoa (or Ectoprocta)

Moss animals, also known as bryozoans (or ectoprocts), are an often misidentified group comprised of nearly 2,000 different species. They live hanging from marine algae, encrusted on rocks and shells, or growing upright from a rock crevice. Tiny individual zooids make up bryozoan colonies. A bryozoan colony comprises hundreds to thousands of individuals. The colony reproduces primarily by asexual budding. Some species are rigid, others flexible and sway in the water, and still others are gelatinous in nature. Bryozoans have a primitive nerve system but lack a circulatory system or excretory system. They feed on minute particles suspended in the water.

Leafy Bryozoan *Flustra foliacea*

Other Name Hornwrack.
Description This species' branches are gray or yellow to tan-colored; their shape is broad, flat, and frequently lobed.
Size To 8" (20 cm) long.
Habitat On rocks and in tidepools; low intertidal zone to depths of 328' (100 m) and more.
Range Arctic to Nova Scotia.
Notes The beige skeletons of leafy bryozoans are frequently found washed ashore after storms. The fronds smell distinctly of lemons when freshly collected. This species resembles an autumn leaf, but a closer look reveals its rectangular compartments. A hand lens greatly aids in viewing these structures. Colonies of leafy bryozoans have been found that are more than 12 years old. This species was unknown on our coast until 1960. The species is also abundant in Europe.

Kelp Encrusting Bryozoan
Membranipora membranacea

Other Names Encrusting bryozoan, lacy-crust bryozoan, kelp lace, coffin bryozoan.
Description Individuals are white and form thin, flat colonies with small rectangular cell-like structures. This species tends to crowd together, radiating from the center.
Size Often exceeds 3" (76 mm) in diameter.
Habitat On seaweeds especially kelp fronds and floats as well as on rocks.
Range Nova Scotia to New Hampshire.
Notes Kelp encrusting bryozoan is an introduced species that favors various species of kelp for attachment. It was introduced into the Gulf of Maine in 1987, and within a mere two years it became the dominant species living on kelps in that area. This species is rapidly spreading and is likely to continue its expansion along the Atlantic coastline. In the Pacific Northwest, where this bryozoan is native, its proliferation is kept in check by two nudibranch species.

Lacy Crust Bryozoans *Electra* spp. and others

Other Names Sea lace, lacy crust.
Description Colony members are white and form a lace-like crust with a box or coffin shape.
Size To 12" (30 cm) in diameter.
Habitat On rocks, shells, seaweeds, and in tidepools; low intertidal zone to deep subtidal depths.
Range The entire coast.
Notes Lacy crust bryozoans include several species that are difficult to identify, even with the help of a microscope. The outline of the colony is normally irregular in shape. Some species harbor sharp spines for protection. They dine on minute creatures suspended in the water. Various nudibranchs feed on these native bryozoans.

Baltic Macoma *Macoma balthica*

MOLLUSCS

Molluscs (or mollusks) include an amazing array of creatures including chitons, limpets, snails, nudibranchs, mussels, clams, and octopus. They are highly diverse, having only a few characteristics in common. All molluscs possess an unsegmented soft body, normally one or more shells to protect the body, a mantle (fold in the body wall that lines the shell), and a muscular foot. The mantle secretes the shells or shell plates. Most possess a radula or file-like feeding structure. Scientists estimate there are some 50,000 to 130,000 species of molluscs in the world—the largest number of species in any single phylum. Most molluscs inhabit marine environments.

Chitons (Class Polyplacophora)

A chiton has 8 overlapping valves or shell plates that are surrounded by a girdle. A large muscular foot is used along with adhesive secretions to cling tightly to a substrate. If it is dislodged from its substrate, it normally rolls into a ball with its plates facing outwards. Most chitons feed on algae and other encrusted foods from the rocks on which they crawl. The radula (tongue) of some chitons has teeth tipped with magnetite, which hardens them. Chitons lack eyes and tentacles, and the sexes are separate. They are found from intertidal levels to waters as deep as 22,960' (7,000 m). Species in this class are often difficult to identify, as they can be very similar in appearance.

White Northern Chiton *Ischnochiton albus*

Other Names White chiton; formerly classified as *Stenosemus albus*.
Description Valves are white occasionally marked with brown; the shell surface is smooth and shows very faint growth lines. The girdle is cream-colored with a granular surface.
Size To 0.5" (13 mm) long.
Habitat On or under rocks; low intertidal zone to depths of 25' (8 m).
Range Arctic to Massachusetts Bay.
Notes Northern white chiton favors the cold waters of northern latitudes and is also found in Alaska's waters. This small species is sometimes observed in the company of northern red chiton (p. 62).

Similar Species **Eastern beaded chiton *Chaetopleura apiculata*,** often referred to as bee chiton, is very similar in size to northern white chiton. It may be encountered from southern Maine to Florida from the very low intertidal zone to subtidal depths. It valves are smooth with 20 longitudinal rows along the surface.

Northern Red Chiton *Tonicella rubra*

Other Names Red chiton, red northern chiton; formerly classified as *Ischnochiton ruber*.
Description A distinctive ridge or keel is present down the middle of the valves. The girdle is covered with tiny elongated scales that do not overlap.
Size To 1" (25 mm) long.
Habitat On and under rocks; low intertidal zone to water 110' (300 m) deep.
Range Arctic to Connecticut.
Notes Northern red chiton is the most common species of chiton encountered in the Atlantic Northeast. It moves slowly in searching of its favorite foods, especially algae. The minute scales on the girdle are visible with a 20x hand lens, an excellent tool for field observations. This species is easily confused with mottled red chiton (below).

Mottled Red Chiton *Tonicella marmorea*

Description This species' dorsal color ranges from tan to reddish brown and is mottled with red or orange. The girdle is smooth (lacking scales or spines), dull, and leather-like. The head valve is flat to slightly convex and a slight ridge is present along the middle.
Size To 1.5" (38 mm) long.
Habitat On rocks; low intertidal zone to subtidal depths of 300' (91 m).
Range Greenland to Massachusetts Bay.

Notes Mottled red chiton feeds on algae, sponges, and hydroids. If you look at the underside of this species, you will find 25 gills present on either side of the foot. Take care to distinguish this species from northern red chiton (above). This species also lives in Europe.

Limpets, Snails, and Allies (Class Gastropoda)

Limpets, snails, and allies are all members of the Class Gastropoda (gastropod means "stomach foot"). Gastropods are a diverse group of invertebrates with few features in common other than a muscular "foot" used for locomotion in most species. In some species, however, this part of the body is modified for swimming or burrowing. Most gastropods have a single, often coiled shell into which their body can withdraw, but this shell is lost or reduced in some groups. Approximately 80% of all molluscs are gastropods. Feeding habits in this group are extremely varied: some are carnivores, while others scavenge, feed on plankton or graze on plant matter. Most species use a radula or rasping tongue to feed. Most gastropods also have a well-developed head that includes eyes, 1–2 pairs of tentacles, and a primitive nervous system.

Diluvian Puncturella *Puncturella noachina*

Other Names Little puncturella, Linne's puncturella, keyhole limpet.
Description The shell exterior is white, and the interior is glossy. A small slit is present in front of the apex with a funnel-shaped hollow around the slit. Radial ribs are also present.
Size To 0.5" (13 mm) long.
Habitat Under rocks; low intertidal zone to depths of 1,800' (548 m).
Range Labrador to Cape Cod, Massachusetts.

Notes Diluvian puncturella is common species that may be found alive in the low intertidal zone or as a shell cast up on the shore. Although its shell is white, it is easily overlooked because of its small size. It feeds on detritus and diatoms that cover the surfaces on which it crawls. This species is also found in the North Pacific.

Tortoiseshell Limpet *Tectura testudinalis*

Other Names Tortoise-shell limpet, common tortoiseshell limpet, plant limpet, Atlantic plate limpet; formerly classified as *Acmaea testudinalis, Notoacmaea testudinalis*.
Description The exterior is gray, often checkered or banded with brown. The interior is bluish with a large chestnut-brown central spot.
Size To 2" (51 mm) long.
Habitat On rocky shores and in tidepools; low intertidal zone to depths of 165' (50 m).
Range Arctic to Long Island Sound.

Notes Identification of this species is easy simply because tortoiseshell limpet is the only limpet commonly found in the Atlantic Northeast. It has a specialized diet, feeding upon encrusting coralline algae, and lives to 3 years. This species is also found along the coast of Europe and the northern Pacific as far south as Alaska.

Spiral Margarite *Margarites helicinus*

Other Names Smooth top shell, smooth helical top shell, helicina margarite.
Description The yellowish-brown translucent shell has an iridescent blue or pinkish-brown finish. The flat shell is smooth with a narrow and deep umbilicus or navel. The inside of the shell is pearly.
Size To 0.33" (8 mm) high.
Habitat On sandy shores; low intertidal zone to depths of 450' (135 m).
Range Arctic to Massachusetts.

Notes This species is found intertidally in the northern portion of it range but deeper in the southern portion. These very small, exquisite snails are gems to view. Its scientific name *helicinus* refers to the spiral nature of its shell. Spiral margarite feeds on algal growth.

Wide Lacuna *Lacuna vincta*

Other Names Common northern chink shell, banded chink shell, chink snail, little chink shell, banded lacuna, northern lacuna.

Description The shell is light brown, often showing 2–4 red-brown bands on the last whorl. A slight depression between columella and inner lip is also present.

Size To 0.6′ (16 mm) high.

Habitat On large seaweed and in tidepools; low intertidal zone to depths of 132′ (40 m).

Range Arctic to Rhode Island.

Notes The shell of wide lacuna is a thin, smooth work of art. This species is able to tolerate salinities as low as 20%. With a lifespan of less than one year, it breads from January through early spring. The distinctive doughnut-shaped egg masses of wide lacuna are laid on seaweed. These eggs hatch into planktonic larvae.

Adults are often found on seaweed.

Egg clusters.

Smooth Periwinkle
Littorina obtusata

Other Names Northern yellow periwinkle, yellow periwinkle, round periwinkle.
Description The shell color varies widely and includes yellow, orange, olive, or brown, often banded. The shell has a low spire and is smooth overall.
Size To .5" (12 mm) high.
Habitat On rocks and seaweeds; low inter-tidal zone.
Range Labrador to New Jersey.

Notes The shells of smooth periwinkles vary greatly in coloration—often bright yellow or orange overall and sometimes also banded. This species is easily distinguished from the other periwinkles of the area by its smooth rounded shell. The similar-looking rough periwinkle displays a distinctive pointed tip on its spire. Common periwinkle (p. 68) also sports a pointed tip to the shell, but it is easily identified by its larger size.

Female smooth periwinkles deposit their eggs on seaweeds or rocks in jelly-like masses. Free-swimming young hatch from these eggs and eventually settle in the intertidal zone, where they spend the remainder of their lives feeding on decaying plant life. This species feeds on knotted wrack (p. 162) and northern rockweed (p. 160). Interestingly enough, knotted wrack can produce noxious chemicals that attract the smooth periwinkle and may repel other periwinkles. The European green crab (p. 125) is this periwinkle's main predator.

Female with eggs.

Rough Periwinkle *Littorina saxatilis*

Other Name Northern rough periwinkle.

Description The shell is yellow, reddish, grayish, or brownish with a pointed spire and smooth spiral cords on convex whorls.

Size To .5" (12 mm) high.

Habitat On rocks and similar locations; high intertidal zone.

Range Arctic to Cape May, New Jersey.

Notes Rough periwinkles are herbivorous, feeding on diatoms, filamentous algae, and plant litter. They also prey upon newly settled barnacles. Unlike

many periwinkles, this species broods its larvae internally, providing them with a nutrient rich home, and then releases them as tiny snails. It can reach maximum densities of well over 100,000 snails per square meter.

Living in the high intertidal zone, rough periwinkles are exposed to air for 70% to 95% of the time. To cope with this situation, they move into crevices and other sheltered areas so as to minimize the effects of desiccation. In air temperatures above 25° Celsius (77° Fahrenheit), these periwinkles lower their metabolic rates; remarkably, they can survive out of water for 42 days!

Common Periwinkle *Littorina littorea*

Other Name Edible periwinkle.

Description Shell is gray to grayish-brown and dark spiral bands are often present. A pointed spire and smooth whorls are distinctive, as are the whitish areas around columella and inside of outer lip.

Size To 1.5" (40 mm) high.

Habitat On rocks and similar surfaces; high to low intertidal zone.

Range Labrador to Virginia.

Notes Although this species was long believed to have been introduced into North American from Europe, recent DNA evidence indicates that it has probably been in North America for at least 8,000 years; it has recently expanded its range southward.

Common periwinkles feed on diatoms, sea lettuce *Ulva* sp. (see p. 149), and laver (p. 164). Females deposit between 10,000 and 100,000 eggs directly into seawater on floating disk-like capsules that eventually disintegrate. The young then enter into a pelagic phase for approximately 6 weeks before settling on solid ground. They reach maturity at 2 or 3 years of age and may live to reach 10 years. The European green

crab (p. 125) is the main predator of the young. This snail was collected as food in England prior to the Second World War. This practice continues today but is uncommon.

Flat Skenea *Skeneopsis planorbis*

Other Names Orb shell, trumpet shell;
formerly *Skenea planorbis*.
Description The reddish brown shell is
flat with coils that rapidly increase in
size. Its umbilicus is wide.
Size To .25" (6 mm) high.
Habitat On seaweed, shells, under rocks
and in tidepools; low intertidal zone to
depths of 96' (32 m).
Range Greenland to Florida.
Notes Due to the small size of this
snail, it often goes unnoticed. The flat

skenea attaches its eggs on filamentous algae. When the young hatch, they do not
go through a free-swimming stage in their development but rather hatch as miniature
adults. This species is also found in Europe.

Brown-band Wentletrap *Epitonium rupicola*

Other Names Brown-
banded wentletrap, lined
wentletrap; formerly classified as *E. lineatum*.
Description The pointed
shell is whitish to yellowish and slender, with many
rounded whorls that hold
10–16 fine axial ribs. Dark
brown bands are often
present.
Size To 1" (25 mm) high.
Habitat In sand of bays
and sounds; low intertidal
zone to depths of 120' (37 m).
Range Cape Cod, Massachusetts to Florida and Texas.

Notes This elegant species
is a predator that feeds
on small anemones. It is
commonly found along
Atlantic coastlines as an
empty shell washed up on
the beach. If irritated, live
wentletraps release a purple
dye from their pigmented
mantle glands as a means of
defense.

Striate Cup-and-saucer *Crucibulum striatum*

Other Names Cup-and-saucer, cup-and-saucer limpet.
Description The shell is white, pink, or yellow on the exterior. Its apex is curved, and the shelf is oval-shaped and attached to side of shell. Axial riblets are found on the exterior.
Size To 1.4" (35 mm) high.
Habitat On rocks, shells and similar objects; low intertidal zone to depths of 1,100' (335 m).
Range Nova Scotia to Florida.
Notes Unlike many gastropods, striate cup-and-saucer obtains its food from the water by filtering minute food particles from the seawater. This species is common from Cape Cod north, becoming increasingly uncommon in the southern portion of its range.

Common Atlantic Slippersnail
Crepidula fornicata

Other Names Boatshell, quarterdeck, common slipper shell.
Description The whitish shell is marked with various brown blotches or stripes, and the interior is white or marked with brown. The inside shelf covers approximately half of the opening.
Size To 2.5" (64 mm) high.

Habitat On rocks, shells or similar objects; low intertidal zone to depths of 50' (15 m).
Range Gulf of St. Lawrence to Florida and Texas.
Notes Several common Atlantic slippersnails are often found stacked on top of one another on a rock or other object. Here smaller individuals (males) are found on top of large individuals (females). In between are the hermaphrodites—those that possess both male and female reproductive organs. This common species is prolific and often found in oyster beds, where it is considered a nuisance.

Eastern White Slippersnail *Crepidula plana*

Other Names Flat slipper, flat slipper shell, eastern white slipper shell.
Description The white shell is flat or near-flat, and the inside shelf covers approximately half of the opening.
Size To 1.6" (41 mm) high.
Habitat On rocks, large shells, or similar objects; low intertidal zone.
Range Gulf of St. Lawrence to Texas.
Notes This species is often found on larger shells such as moon snails. If it grows on the inside of these shells, its shape is modified into one that grows "inside-out." It has also been found living on the shells of crabs. This species does not pile up as common Atlantic slippersnail (p. 70) does.

American Pelicanfoot *Aporrhais occidentalis*

Other Name American pelican's foot.
Description Shell is gray to yellowish overall, and the outer lip is extended into a large wing-like projection.
Size To 2.5" (64 mm) high.
Habitat In mud or sand; from 30' (9 m) to depths of 1,800' (549 m).
Range Labrador to North Carolina.

Notes The remarkable shell of American pelicanfoot is unique in the North Atlantic—the only member of its family (Aporrhaidae) found in the region. The shells of this species are sometimes found washed up on the beach. This snail is found in very deep waters in the southern part of its range. The large wing-like projection is smaller in young specimens. This species is occasionally found in the stomachs of fish.

71

Lobed Moonsnail *Neverita duplicata*

Other Names Shark eye; also classified as *N. duplicatus* and *Polinices duplicata*.

Description The slate gray to tan shell is globe-shaped with 4–5 body whorls. Its spire is very low, flat, and rounded. A thick, dark brown callus nearly covers the umbilicus. The tentacles are yellow with a black stripe.

Size To 3" (76 mm) high, 3.75" (95 mm) wide.

Habitat In sand or muddy sand; low intertidal zone to shallow depths.

Range Cape Cod, Massachusetts to Florida and Texas.

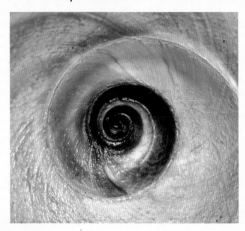

Notes Lobed moonsnail is a predator of snails and clams. It dines on many species, including blue mussel, northern horsemussel, Atlantic surfclam, Arctic wedgeclam, Atlantic jackknifeclam, northern quahog, and soft-shell-clam. Like all moonsnails, it completely envelops its prey (if small enough) with its large foot to drill a round, beveled hole into the shell of its prey using its radula. It also adds an acid to further dissolve the shell. It then releases digestive enzymes into the prey to aid it in sucking out its partially digested meal.

Egg case.

Northern Moonsnail *Euspira heros*

Other Names Common northern moon-shell; formerly classified as *Natica heros* and *Lunatia heros*.

Description The slate gray to tan shell is globe-shaped with 4–5 body whorls. Its spire is low and rounded. A callus is absent, and the umbilicus is large, round, and deep. Its tentacles are yellow.

Size To 5″ (12.7 cm) high.

Habitat In sand; low intertidal zone to depths of 1,200′ (366 m).

Range Labrador to North Carolina.

Notes Much like lobed moonsnail (see above), northern moonsnail is a predator of bivalves. Beachcombers may find empty shells on the beach or observe live individuals at the surface of the sand or buried to a depth of 6″ (15 cm) from the surface. This large species is found in deeper waters in the southern portion of its range. Females lay distinctive egg collars from May to September, each containing several thousand eggs. These hatch and produce tiny planktonic larvae. Their large egg collars provide food for other gastropods and green sea urchins (p. 136). Moonsnails

grow slowly, and it is thought that their age can be estimated by counting the rings on their operculum. The accuracy of this ageing technique, however, has not been verified.

Spotted Moonsnail *Euspira triseriata*

Other Names Spotted northern
moon-shell, spotted moon shell;
formerly classified as *Lunatia
triseriata*.
Description The buff-colored
shell hosts three rows of purplish
or brownish square-shaped spots.
Size To 1" (25 mm) high.
Habitat On sandy bottoms; in
subtidal waters 6–350' (1.8–107
m) deep.
Range Labrador to North Carolina;
uncommon south of Cape Cod.
Notes The small and beautiful
shell of spotted moonsnail is sometimes found washed up on the beach after a storm.
Spotted moonsnails sometimes lack spots on their shells, and as a result these individuals are mistaken for juvenile northern moonsnails (p. 73).

Atlantic Oyster Drill *Urosalpinx cinerea*

Description The spindle-shaped shell is gray to yellowish-white, often with brownish
spiral bands. The inside aperture is often purple. A total of 9–12 low vertical folds are
found on each whorl. There are 2–6 small teeth inside, and the outer lip is sometimes
thickened.
Size To 1.75" (4.4 cm) high.
Habitat On rocks, in oyster beds, and in similar areas in the sheltered waters of bays
and similar areas; mid-intertidal zone to depths of 50' (15 m).
Range Gulf of St. Lawrence to northern Florida.
Notes Atlantic oyster drill was introduced from Europe over 100 years ago. As the
common name suggests, this species is a major predator of young eastern oysters (p.
96). Atlantic oyster drill and thick-lip drill (p. 76) cannot tolerate low salinity; as a
result, commercial oyster farmers locate their oyster beds in low-salinity areas, such
as river mouths, to avoid both predators.

Females are active
all summer, laying
their vase-shaped
eggs on rocks or
other hard objects.
Larvae crawl from
these eggs within 6
to 8 weeks. Young
snails emerge
as well-formed
miniature adults to
begin their lives as
predators.

Atlantic Dogwinkle *Nucella lapillus*

Other Names Dogwinkle; also classified as *Thais lapillus*.

Description Shell varies widely from white to orange and brown to black, often with spiral stripes. The aperture is oval with a thick outer lip.

Size To 2" (51 mm) high.

Habitat On rocks and similar hard objects; high to low intertidal zone.

Range Labrador to Long Island Sound.

Notes Atlantic dogwinkle shells vary greatly with an exterior that is knobby, scaly, or smooth, but individuals living near or below the low tide mark typically have shells that are smooth because there is less wave action there. The coloration also varies widely, including white, yellow,

pink, lavender, orange, brown or black. This species feeds on young mussels, clams, or barnacles. Diet has been found to influence the color of its shell: dark individuals are so pigmented because they eat mostly blue mussels. Females lay their eggs in vase-shaped capsules that are positioned on long stalks. These capsules are placed on the undersides of rocks. From there, the young emerge as miniature adults. In times past, Native North American peoples obtained a purple dye from dogwinkles.

Egg capsules.

Thick-lip Drill *Eupleura caudata*

Other Names Thick-lipped drill, thick-lipped oyster drill.
Description The shell exterior is gray, and the inside aperture is often purple. The shell is spindle-shaped with angled "shoulders" on whorls and a long tubular anterior canal. Enlarged axial ribs are located beside and across from the aperture.

Size To 1.6" (4.1 cm) high.
Habitat On oyster beds, jetties, and pilings in the sheltered waters of bays and similar areas; mid-intertidal zone to depths of approximately 50' (15 m).
Range Cape Cod, Massachusetts to Florida.
Notes This small predator is easily confused

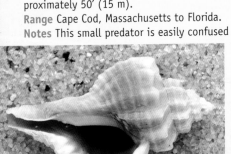

with the similar oyster drill (p. 74). As its common name suggests, this species has a thickened outer lip.

This predator feeds on young oysters by drilling a small hole into the oyster shell and inserting its proboscis (long "snout") to suck out the soft tissue inside. It also feeds on barnacles and snails. Females lay their eggs in distinctive shield-shaped capsules that are positioned on the top of slender stalks.

Lunar Dovesnail *Astyris lunata*

Other Names Lunar dove-shell, chink shell, crescent mitrella; formerly classified as *Mitrella lunata*.
Description The yellowish to brown or gray shell is smooth and translucent. Brown crescent-shaped or zig-zag markings are also present. Four small teeth are found inside the outer lip.

Size To 0.25" (6 mm) high.
Habitat On mud bottoms, among seaweed and eelgrass; low intertidal zone to shallow subtidal depths.
Range Maine to Florida and Texas.
Notes This minute species is commonly found clinging to rocks and shell fragments in quiet waters of bays and similar areas. The translucent shell of lunar dovesnail is brightly colored when wet.

Waved Whelk *Buccinum undatum*

Other Names Common northern whelk, common northern buccinum, edible whelk.
Description The shell is yellowish-white with 6 round whorls. A total of 9–15 prominent slanted, raised ribs are present and crossed by fine threads between.
Size To 5.5" (14 cm) high.
Habitat On rocky and sandy shores; low intertidal zone to depths of 200' (61 m).
Range Labrador to New Jersey.
Notes Waved whelk is a scav-

enger that feeds on many creatures, including green sea urchins, fish eggs, crabs, and trematodes. Its enemies include various sea stars. Their distinctive egg cases, which can often be found washed up on the beach, may be 3" (cm) in diameter and are often compared to a cluster of Rice Krispies. These egg cases were once called "sea wash balls" because they were used by mariners to wash their hands. Waved whelks are also found in European waters, where they grow to a larger size.

Stimpson Whelk *Colus stimpsoni*

Other Names Stimpson's colus, Stimpson's spindle shell.
Description The shell is yellowish to gray and spindle-shaped with an extended spire. Faint spiral threads are present with a thin brown periostracum (paper-like covering).
Size To 5" (12.7 cm) high.
Habitat In sand, mud, or clay; from depths of 5' (1.5 m) to 2,800' (853 m).
Range Labrador to Cape Hatteras.

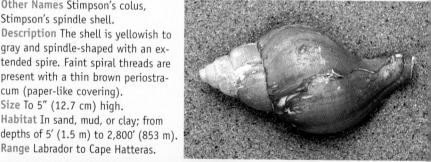

Notes Although Stimpson whelks do not live on intertidal beaches, their distinctive shells can frequently be found washed up onshore, especially in the Cape Cod region. The species prefers colder waters, as indicated by the amazing depths at which it lives.

Ten-ridged Whelk *Neptunea lyrata decemcostata*

Other Names Corded Neptune, wrinkle whelk, New England ten-ridge whelk, New England neptune; formerly classified as *Neptunea decemcostata*.
Description The shell is grayish overall with 7 to 10 strong brown chords on the body whorl and 2 to 3 on upper whorls.
Size To 5" (12.7 cm) high.
Habitat On rocky bottoms; from depths of 60' (18 m) to 300' (91m).
Range Newfoundland to southern Massachusetts.

Notes As with several other whelks, ten-ridged whelk lives in subtidal environments. Its shells are often found washed ashore, especially after storms. The beautiful shells are distinctive and make identification rather easy. This species is occasionally found by fishermen in their lobster pots.

Three-lined Basketsnail *Nassarius trivittatus*

Other Names Three-lined Basket shell, three-lined mud snail, threeline mudsnail, New England dog whelk, New England nassa; also classified as *Ilyanassa trivittata* and *Nassa trivittatus*.
Description The light brown to yellowish shell is spindle-shaped with deep sutures. The shell is also detailed with equal-sized spiral lines and ribs, creating a bead-like finish. The body is whitish with light violet spots.
Size To 0.75" (19 mm) high.
Habitat On sand or sandy mud; low intertidal zone to depths of 270' (82 m).
Range Nova Scotia to Florida.
Notes The delicate beaded detail on the shell of this snail is best viewed with a hand lens of 10X or stronger. This small species is found in quiet sheltered waters, where

it feeds on dead organisms and the egg collars the northern moonsnail (see p. 73). The underside of these egg collars also provides an excellent site for it to lay its eggs.

Knobbed Whelk *Busycon carica*

Description The shell
is gray to pale brown
overall with a spindle-
shape. The body whorl
is narrowed gradually
with a wide open canal.
Distinct knobs are pres-
ent on the "shoulders"
and spire.
Size To 9" (23 cm) high.
Habitat On sandy
shores; low intertidal
zone to depths of 15'
(4.6 m).
Range Cape Cod,
Massachusetts to Cape
Canaveral, Florida.

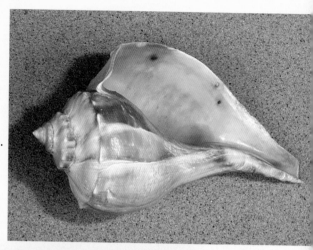

Notes After
a storm, the
dead shells of
knobbed whelks
are often found
cast up on the
shore. During
low tides live in-
dividuals may be
found buried in
the sand where
their main food
item, clams,
are found. Most
knobbed whelk
shells are dextral
in nature or coiled in a right-handed (clockwise)
direction. Some specimens have been collected
(offshore from southern New Jersey) that are
sinistral shells, that is, coiled in a left-handed
(counter-clockwise) direction. These shells are
unusual and prized by collectors. Knobbed whelk
is one of three species of whelks commercially
harvested in the United States. Females lay
their distinctive eggs near the low tide line.
Their eggs may be described as a stack of check-
ers (with jagged, somewhat squared edges) in
an accordion-like belt.

Egg case.

79

Channeled Whelk *Busycotypus canaliculatus*

Other Name Formerly classified as *Busycon canaliculatum*.

Description The shell is gray to yellowish overall with a spindle-shape. The body whorl is narrowed abruptly with a long and narrow open canal. The sutures are channeled between whorls.

Size To 8" (20 cm) high.

Habitat In sand or mud shores; low intertidal zone to shallow subtidal depths.

Range Cape Cod, Massachusetts to northern Florida.

Notes Its always a treat to find the large shell of the channeled whelk or knobbed whelk (see p. 79) at the beach. Both species may be found stranded after a storm in the Cape Cod area.

Channeled whelk is a predator, feeding primarily on bivalves such as clams. It feeds by thrusting its aperture canal ("nose") between the shells of its prey. The clam reacts by closing its valves tightly, which breaks a shell, allowing the snail to feed on the soft body tissue inside. This whelk is also a scavenger and is often attracted to the bait used in lobster pots. The females lay eggs that resemble a stack of miniature compact discs (with thin edges) in an accordion-like belt. These egg cases are often found washed up on the beach.

Egg case.

Eastern Mud Snail *Ilyanassa obsoleta*

Other Names Eastern mud whelk, eastern mud nassa, black dog whelk, mud dog whelk, worn out dog whelk; formerly classified as *I. obsoletus* and *Nassarius obsoletus*.

Description Shell is dark brown to black, sometimes with a white spiral band. It is spindle-shaped with 6 whorls, a blunt end (often eroded), and several spiral threads. A greenish color is sometimes present due to micro-scopic algae.

Size To 1.1" (3 cm) high.

Habitat On mud flats; low intertidal zone to just below it.

Range Gulf of St. Lawrence to Florida.

Notes Eastern mud snail feeds on both organic material and carrion and buries itself in the mud when the tide goes out. Under the right conditions it can be found in accumulations numbering into the thousands. It is thought to have a life span of 5 years. This species has been introduced to the Pacific coast. Dark individuals are probably the least attractive of the snails found along North American coasts.

Solitary Bubble *Haminoea solitaria*

Other Names Solitary glassy bubble, solitary paper bubble, Say's paper bubble.

Description The shell color ranges from bluish white to yellowish brown. Spiral scratch-like markings are found on the surface of the ovoid shell.

Size To 0.5" (13 mm) long.

Habitat On mud flats; low intertidal zone to depths of 30' (9 m).

Range Cape Cod, Massa-chusetts to North Carolina.

Notes Solitary bubble is a gray, slug-like creature. This hermaphroditic spe-cies has a large foot that is used to burrow in the mud about a half inch (1 cm) below the surface. The soft body of this crea-ture covers much of its extremely fragile shell.

Nudibranchs (Subclass Opisthobranchia)

The nudibranchs or "sea slugs" are favorites of divers, beachcombers, and snorkelers because many of them display such spectacular colors and patterns. Others have coloring that allows them to match their environment very closely. Nudibranchs are gastropods that shed their shell when they are young to become shell-less as adults. They are renowned for their vibrant colors, fantastical shapes, and mysterious fluctuations in population. Many nudibranchs have chemical defenses or discharge stinging cells called nematocysts. Predators of nudibranchs are few. All nudibranchs have a pair of intricate projections near the head, called rhinophores, which help them detect chemicals in the water. Some of these chemicals can help lead the nudibranch to food sources.

White Atlantic Cadlina *Cadlina laevis*

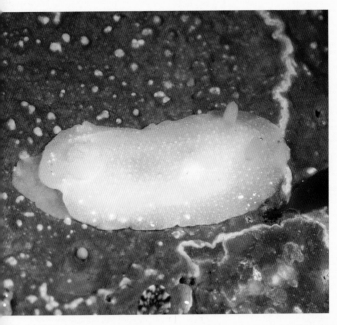

Description The oval body is translucent white with yellow speckles overall. A ring of yellow-tipped feathery gills grace the posterior end, and the coil-like rhinophores are translucent.
Size To 1.25" (30 mm) long.
Habitat On rocky shores and in tidepools; low intertidal zone to depths of 2,624' (800 m).
Range Arctic to Massachusetts.
Notes Yellow-tipped poison glands grace the surface of this beautiful nudibranch. White Atlantic cadlina produces large eggs that hatch directly into miniature nudibranchs that do not require a planktonic stage in their development. Food for the larvae is included inside the eggs; in other nudibranchs, young forage for food in the plankton. Slime sponges provide the food necessary for this species once they have finished the food inside the eggs.

Barnacle-eating Dorid *Onchidoris bilamellata*

Other Names Barnacle-eating onchidoris, barnacle-eating nudibranch, rough-mantled nudibranch, rough-mantled doris; formerly classified as *O. fusca*.
Description The body is cream-colored to reddish-brown overall and covered with short tubercles. A circle of 16 to 32 gills grace the rear.
Size To 1.5" (40 mm) long.
Habitat Under rocks; low intertidal zone.
Range Arctic to Rhode Island.
Notes Just as its name suggests, an adult barnacle-eating dorid feeds exclusively upon barnacles, although juveniles have been shown to feed upon encrusting bryozoans. Looking under rocks, the beachcomber often discovers the distinctive white egg clusters of this species clinging to the undersides of rocks. The adults are often beside them, guarding their eggs. This nudibranch is an annual

Adults guarding eggs.

species that is often found in the presence of the hairy spiny doris (below).

Hairy Spiny Doris *Onchidoris*

Other Name Hairy Doris.
Description The body is white, yellow, orange, mauve, or dark brown overall. The dorsal surface is covered in soft tubercles with a circle of up to 9 tri-pinnate gills that grace its rear.
Size To 2.2" (55 mm) long.
Habitat Under rocks on protected shores; mid-intertidal zone to depths of 558' (170 m).
Range Nova Scotia to Virginia.

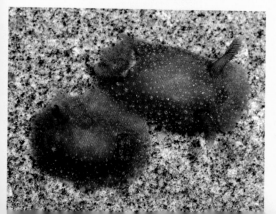

Notes This delightful, relatively common species is often found sporting several colorations at the same location. It feeds on a variety of encrusting bryozoans. The hairy spiny doris is also present in Europe, where researchers have observed two separate spawning seasons, in spring and autumn. Researchers believe that this nudibranch likely lives less than 2 years. Doris is the name of a Greek goddess.

83

Fuzzy Onchidoris *Onchidoris muricata*

Other Names White dorid, muricate doris; formerly classified as *O. aspera, O. hystricina,* and *O. varians.*
Description The body is white to yellow overall, and the dorsal area is covered in flat-topped tubercles.
Size To 0.5" (14 mm) long.
Habitat Beneath rocks; low intertidal zone to depths of 200' (60 m).
Range Nova Scotia to Connecticut.
Notes The metamorphosis of the fuzzy onchidoris is truly remarkable. Adults lay up to 50,000 small eggs before dying. These eggs hatch into veliger larvae that take on a pelagic (open-ocean) lifestyle. These tiny young drift in search of their food, two species of bryozoans: lacy crust bryozoans (p. 59) and kelp encrusting bryozoan (p. 59). If either of these foods are not found, they perish. When they do settle on either food source, chemical signals are received from the bryozoan, and several changes occur. These larvae transform from swimmers into crawlers by enlarging their muscular foot and permanently losing their shell in the process. They also change the way they feed from using cilia or tiny hair-like fingers into rasping and sucking techniques. And so the change occurs only for those that find either food.

This species is widely distributed in the northern hemisphere, where it can be found in Europe, Russia, Iceland, Greenland, and in the Pacific from Alaska to California.

Similar Species Yellow false doris *Adalaria proxima* is virtually identical in appearance except that it is often yellowish, larger—reaching .6" (17 mm) long—and its tubercles are pointed. Its radulae or teeth are much different as well, but a microscope is needed to verify the differences. The egg mass of yellow false doris is much smaller, reaching only 2,000 large eggs.

Atlantic Ancula *Ancula gibbosa*

Other Name Also classified as *A. cristata*.

Description The body is white or translucent white overall, with orange or yellow tips of tubercles. Orange is often present on tips of gills and rhinophores (large tentacles on head). A circle of feather-like gills on the back surround the anus.

Size To 1.25" (33 mm) long.

Habitat On rocks and seaweeds; low intertidal zone to depths of 330' (100 m).

Range Arctic to Massachusetts.

Notes This dainty species is often found under rocks where several individuals may live together. The transparent body of Atlantic ancula reveals its internal organs rather nicely. In Connecticut this species spawns from April to June. It has been collected from May to late August in Nova Scotia, and egg masses have been found from June through August.

The food of Atlantic ancula appears to be bit of a mystery. Its prey species have been identified at various locations to include a white sponge, a colonial bryozoan, and two tunicates. Other researchers believe it is a herbivore. More research is needed to clarify this species' natural history, including its food habits.

Bushy-backed Nudibranch
Dendronotus frondosus

Other Names Frond-aeolis, bushy-backed sea slug, leafy dendronotid; formerly classified as *D. arborescens, D. venustus,* and *Amphitrite frondosa*.

Description The body is white to yellow, mottled or banded with red or brown. A row of branched cerata or projections are present along the back.

Size To 1.25" (30 mm) long for intertidal specimens; to 4.6" (117 mm) long for subtidal individuals.

Habitat On rocks, hydroid colonies, seaweed, and in tidepools; low intertidal zone to depths of 1,320' (400 m).

Range Arctic to New Jersey.

Notes The bushy-backed nudibranch may be found in a wide variety of colors. It has been documented that this predator changes its feeding habits to different hydroid species as it grows larger. Several studies have been conducted on this species. Its

lifespan has been estimated to reach 3 months by some researchers, while others suggest a lifespan of 2 years is more likely. It likely reproduces year-round, as its round egg masses have been found in the colder and warmer months of the year.

Dwarf Balloon Aeolis *Eubranchus pallidus*

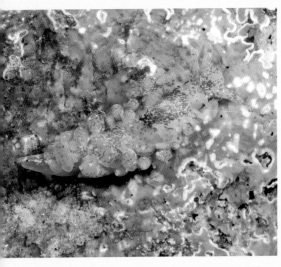

Other Names Club-gilled nudibranch; formerly classified as *E. exiguus.*
Description The translucent orange body is highlighted with orange, gold, or reddish spots. Two pairs of tentacles are present, and the dorsal cerata are large and inflated.
Size To 0.75" (20 mm) long.
Habitat On rocks and seaweeds; low intertidal zone to subtidal depths.
Range Arctic to Massachusetts.
Notes The dwarf balloon aeolis is an elegant species that feeds on a variety of hydroid species. As its common name suggests, it is a small species with balloon-shaped projections attached to its dorsal surface. This uncommon species is also found in Europe.

Graceful Aeolis *Flabellina gracilis*

Other Name Formerly *Coryphella gracilis.*
Description Translucent white overall. The cerata are orange to crimson with a white ring at the translucent tip. Clustered white flecks are present on the dorsal side of oral tentacles and the tip of the tail. The cerata are present in several clusters, but the space between clusters is reduced. This species also has a "notched head" when viewed from above.
Size To 0.5" (12 mm) long.
Habitat On rocky shores and in tidepools; low intertidal zone to depths of 100' (33 m).

Range Nova Scotia to Cape Cod, Massachusetts.
Notes The graceful aeolis closely resembles the much smaller red-finger aeolis (p. 87). A close examination is needed to identify this species correctly. This nudibranch feeds exclusively upon hydroids and reproduces at least twice each year. It is also found in Europe.

Red-finger Aeolis *Flabellina verrucosa*

Other Names
Red-finger
nudibranch,
red-gilled nudi-
branch; formerly
classified as
*Coryphella
verrucosa*.
Description
Translucent
white overall.
The cerata are
red to brown
with a white
ring at the
translucent tip.
A white line

extends along the tail into the last few cerata, and a narrow white line is present on the dorsal side of oral tentacles. The cerata are in several clusters and the front edge of foot extended at the sides.

Size To 1.33" (35 mm) long.

Habitat On rocks, seaweed, or in tidepools; low intertidal zone to depths of 1,312' (400 m).

Range Labrador to the Gulf of Maine.

The cerata of red-finger aeolis are present in several clusters—each with a translucent tip and a white ring.

Notes The color in this species and other aeolids is very often a result of the color of their food, which accumulates in the ducts of their digestive gland. These are located in the cerata or finger-like projections on their dorsal surface. The red-finger aeolis is the most common of several similar intertidal aeolids that have long been confused with each other.

Similar Species Graceful aeolis *F. gracilis* (p. 86) is a smaller species reaching 0.5" (12 mm) with white-tipped cerata and more distinctly arranged rows. This species also has a "notched" appearance to the head.

Salmon aeolis *F. salmonacea* is, as its name suggests, bright salmon-colored. Its cerata form one continuous cluster. The tips of its cerata are translucent with a white ring. This large species grows to reach 1.5" (40 mm) in length.

Shag-rug Nudibranch *Aeolidia papillosa*

Other Names Shag-rug aeolis, maned nudibranch.
Description This species' body is brown to pale orange, and the sides are covered with finger-like cerata (projections).
Size To .5" (12 cm) long.
Habitat On protected rocky shores and tidepools; mid-intertidal zone to depths of 2,624' (800 m).
Range Arctic to Maryland.

Notes The shag-rug nudibranch dines on sea anemones. The short plumose anemone (p. 34) provides the main source of food for this appropriately named nudibranch. It feeds at least once a day, consuming up to 100% of its body weight. In order for this nudibranch to feed on anemones, it must first become immune to the stinging cells (nematocysts) on the anemone tentacles. Apparently, the nudibranch first touches the anemone, then retreats, which activates the production of a coating resistant to the stinging effects. The shag-rug nudibranch can then feed on the anemone without becoming a meal in itself.

Clams and Allies (Class Bivalvia)

Bivalves are molluscs that are covered by a pair of shells (valves). This large class contains about 12,000 species worldwide, including mussels, oysters, clams, scallops, and shipworms. Some live in fresh water, but most are found in saltwater environments, buried in sand and mud (clams), on rock (piddocks), and in wood (shipworms). Others have evolved to become mobile and capable of swimming (scallops). Bivalves have come to occupy very diverse environments but have remained relatively unchanged over millions of years.

Clams feed, breathe, and expel wastes through siphons, special tubes that extend from the clam to the surface. Oxygen passes into the blood while water flows over the gills. At the same time tiny food particles are trapped by sticky mucus which eventually is transferred to the mouth. Many species of bivalves are eaten by humans.

Boreal Awningclam *Solemya borealis*

Other Names Northern awningclam, northern veiled clam.
Description The exterior of the thin smooth shells covered in a thick brown membranous periostracum. The interior of the elongated shells are grayish blue.
Size To 3" (75 mm) long.
Habitat In sand; in subtidal depths.
Range Nova Scotia to Connecticut.
Notes A skin-like periostracum overhangs the outside edge of the shell from which its name, awningclam, arises. The fragile nature of this common species is readily apparent. In fact, it can be difficult to find an unbroken shell. This subtidal species is often found washed up on shore after a storm. Its siphon openings are adorned with about 40 finger-like projections. Boreal awningclam is capable of swimming in short, jet-propelled spurts.

File Yoldia *Yoldia limatula*

Description The exterior of the shells are white, covered with a shiny greenish to chestnut-brown periostracum. The rear of each shell tapers gradually, and the front is rounded. Approximately 30 teeth are found on the inside edge of the shell in front of the umbo and about 26 behind the umbo. A small chondrophore (spoon-shaped projection) is present on one shell.
Size To 2.5" (64 mm) long.
Habitat In mud and sandy mud sites; low intertidal zone to depths of 100′ (30 m).
Range Gulf of St. Lawrence to New Jersey.
Notes File yoldia bears several file-like teeth on the inside edge of its shells. This species is reported to be quite active and able to leap with its foot using sudden thrusts. It is commonly found in bays and estuaries. There are also other very similar species with fewer teeth on the edge of the shell, but this is the most common species encountered in the Atlantic Northeast.

Transverse Ark *Anadara transversa*

Other Name Formerly classified as *Arca transversa*.

Description The sturdy white shells are covered with a brown, hairy periostracum (skin-like covering). They are rectangular in shape, with the ribs on the right valve normally beaded and rarely on the left. The ligament is long and wide.

Size To 1.5" (40 mm) long.

Habitat In sandy or muddy bottoms; in waters 3.3–36' (1–11 m) deep.

Range Massachusetts to Florida and Texas.

Notes Transverse arks are sometimes found washed upon the beach after storms. Its hairy periostracum is often worn away as a result of the abrasion of the sand and waves.

Blood Ark *Anadara ovalis*

Other Names Bloody clam; formerly classified as *A. pexata* and *Arca pexata*.

Description The oval-shaped shells are white with a brown, hairy periostracum (skin-like covering); the ligament is narrow.

Size To 3" (7.6 cm) long.

Habitat In sandy or muddy bottoms; low intertidal zone to depths of 10' (3 m).

Range Cape Cod, Massachusetts to Brazil.

Notes Aptly named, the blood of blood ark is red, which indicates the presence of the red respiratory pigment hemoglobin. Most molluscs have blood that is clear or light blue in color. The hemoglobin of this species has been used to study the properties of human hemoglobin, including fluorescence.

Blue Mussel *Mytilus edulis*

Other Name Edible mussel.
Description The shells of adults are a dark blue to black, whereas juveniles are often brighter blue to brown.
Size To 4" (102 mm) long.
Habitat On rocks and similar hard objects; high intertidal zone to depths of 200' (60 m).
Range Arctic to South Carolina.
Notes The tasty blue mussel is often served at seafood restaurants. This common and widespread bivalve anchors to a large rock or other solid object with its byssus (thread-like fibers) that is secreted by a special gland on the foot. Hundreds of blue mussels

may cover a square yard (or meter) of rock completely. If blue mussels are anchored in an intertidal site, they wait until the ocean covers them to feed. In order to feed, they pass water through their mantle cavity, where they filter out tiny food particles that are suspended in the water. Their enemies are numerous and include sea stars, moonsnails, gulls, sea ducks, and humans. Indeed, this is a very important species in the food chain of many marine species.

Blue mussels are relatively slow growing in the wild. It often takes 7–12 years for them to obtain a length of 2.5" (6.5 cm). In the wild, mussels live about 12 years, although a few individuals have been recorded over 24 years old.

Northern Horsemussel *Modiolus modiolus*

Other Names Atlantic modiolus, bearded mussel, horse mussel; formerly classified as *Volsella modiolus*.

Description The dull white shells are covered in brown to purplish-black flaky periostracum. Orange soft tissue is protected inside the heavy shells, which have a narrow front end and wider rear end.

Size To 7" (18 cm) long.
Habitat Buried in gravel or rocks; low intertidal zone to depths of 660' (200 m).
Range Arctic to Florida.
Notes Unlike most mussels, northern horsemussels can burrow. They often cluster together in groups. Their byssus (thread-like fibers) attaches to the surrounding rock and to other horsemussels, helping them to stay in place. This mussel is circumpolar in distribution. Unlike many other bivalves, it is not considered palatable.

Ribbed Mussel *Geukensia demissa*

Other Names Ribbed horse mussel, ribbed horsemussel, Atlantic ribbed mussel, northern ribbed mussel; formerly classified as *Mytilus demissus, Modiola plicatula*, and *Modiola semicostata*.

Description The elongated shells are covered in a yellowish-brown to black periostracum (covering), which is often worn through in spots to reveal the gray or silvery shell. Prominent radiating ribs are found on the shells' exterior.

Size To 5" (12.7 cm) long.
Habitat Partially buried in mud or attached to pilings salt marshes and bays; high to mid-intertidal zones.
Range Gulf of St. Lawrence to Florida and Texas.
Notes This species positions itself in the mud so that the upper halves of its valves (shells) are exposed. Ribbed mussels are not hermaphroditic, and their sex can be determined by the color of the mantle. Males tend to have yellowish-cream shells, whereas females are normally medium brown. Most bivalves only consume phytoplankton, but ribbed mussels are one of the few bivalves able to forage on smaller bacterioplankton. This species has an amazingly high range of tolerances, including dehydration, temperatures as high as 133° F (56° C), and salinities twice that of normal seawater.

93

Bay Scallop *Argopecten irradians*

Other Names Atlantic bay
scallop; formerly classified as
Aequipecten irradians.

Description The exterior of the
shells are white to dark brown
with concentric colored bands or
rays; the lower valve is normally
lighter in color. There are 17–18
prominent radial ribs with large
and equal ears.

Size To 3″ (7.6 cm) wide.

Habitat In muddy sand with eelgrass; low intertidal zone to depths
of 60′ (18 m).

Range Cape Cod, Massachusetts
to Florida and Texas.

Notes Bay scallop is harvested
commercially but is becoming
scarce due to overfishing and
the reduction in eelgrass beds.
This species can move rapidly
underwater by using its adductor muscle. It also has 30 to 40

bright blue eyes that are capable of detecting movement. Beachcombers, however,
rarely find live bay scallops, though their shells can be found on a beach after a
storm.

Sea Scallop *Placopecten magellanicus*

Other Names Deep sea scallop, Atlantic deep sea scallop, giant scallop.
Description The exterior of left valve is gray to reddish-brown, while the right is dirty white in color. There are many fine radial threads on the almost circular valves, and the front ear is slightly larger the than rear.
Size To 8" (20 cm) wide.
Habitat On sand or gravel bottoms; in water 12–400' (4–122 m) deep.
Range Labrador to Cape Hatteras.
Notes This delectable species supports the largest scallop fishery in North America. Its large, impressive shells are sometimes found along Atlantic shorelines.

Common Jingle *Anomia simplex*

Other Names Common jingle shell, jingle shell, toenail shell.
Description The shells have a white, yellow, orange, or black exterior and are thin and circular, with three muscle scars on the left valve.
Size To 2.25" (5.7 cm) high.
Habitat On rocks, wharves, or similar objects; low intertidal zone to depths of 30' (9 m).
Range Nova Scotia to Brazil.
Notes Jingle shells are thin and distinctive, with a prominent hole found on the inside shell where the animal attaches itself to a rock with its byssus (thread-like fibers). The outer or left shell is thicker, rounded and more likely to be found washed up on shore after a storm. The living bivalve may be found attached to the underside or overhang of a large rock at a low tide.
Similar Species Prickly Jingle *A. squamula* is a smaller species, reaching 0.75" (19 mm) high, that can be found in northern waters from Labrador to North Carolina. Its outer valve has rough, prickly scales, while its left valve displays two muscle scars.

Eastern Oyster *Crassostrea virginica*

Other Names Atlantic oyster, common oyster, American oyster, gulf coast oyster.
Description Shells have a dull whitish exterior and glossy white interior with a variable shape and a single purple muscle scar.
Size To 10" (25 cm) long.
Habitat On rocks; low intertidal zone to depths of 40' (12 m).
Range Gulf of St. Lawrence to Florida and Texas.

Notes Oysters have been a delight to the palette for centuries, beginning with the Roman emperors, who paid for them by their weight in gold. All oysters, including the eastern oyster, are thought to have aphrodisiac powers. Research into the aphrodisiac qualities of bivalve molluscs, including those of mussels and clams, has detected two relatively rare amino acids in the bivalves. These amino acids were shown to trigger a chain reaction of hormones that ended with the production of testosterone in males and progesterone in females. Although these studies were conducted in rats, it is likely that similar biochemical reactions occur in humans. Because cooking reduces the quantity of these amino acids, oysters would presumably have to be eaten raw to be most effective. Oysters contain a large amount of zinc, a building block of testosterone. So oysters may indeed be the aphrodisiac that some have considered a myth.

Eastern oysters are protandric: in the first year, they start out as males, but as they grow larger and develop more energy reserves, they change into females. Although large female oysters may release more than 100 million eggs during a season, only about one percent of the fertilized eggs reach the next stage of maturity. Feeding on plankton and algae, the larvae, each about the size of a grain of pepper, go through several stages to reach the settling stage called "spat."

Adult eastern oysters contend with several predators. Several species of crabs can crack the shells to feed upon the meat of the oyster. Atlantic oyster drills (p. 74) can rasp a hole through the shell and insert its tubular proboscis to reach the soft flesh inside. Boreing sponges (p. 27) burrow into the valves and in the process riddles the valves with extensive burrows in live and dead oyster shells. Sea stars are also predators that use their tube feet to clamp onto the shells and pry open them to remove the fresh meal inside. Eastern oysters are plagued by several diseases and

have declined throughout their range in recent times.

Occasionally, sand grains or other particles find their way into the mantle tissue. The mantle tissue secretes a protective covering around it that eventually forms a "pearl." This species' pearls are of no commercial value, however, because commercial oysters lack the ingredient in its secretion to form the mother-of-pearl coating of the true pearl.

Northern Cyclocardia *Cyclocardia borealis*

Other Names Northern cardia, heartclam, northern heart shell; formerly classified as *Venericardia borealis*.

Description The species has white shells with a rusty brown periostracum and 15–20 beaded, radiating ribs.

Size To 1.5" (3.8 cm) high.

Habitat In sand, gravel, or under stones; in water 15–750' (4.6–229 m) deep.

Range Labrador to North Carolina.

Notes The valves of this species are often found on the beach with their felt-like periostracum (skin-like covering) worn off, revealing the white shell beneath. This species is an important food source for several bottom-feeding fish.

Smooth Astarte *Astarte castanea*

Other Names Chestnut astarte, castanet shell.

Description The triangular shells are white with fine concentric ridges; the periostracum (skin-like covering) is a light brown to chestnut brown.

Size To 1.25" (3.2 cm) high.

Habitat In mud or muddy sand; in subtidal waters 25–100' (7.6–30 m) deep.

Range Nova Scotia to New Jersey.

Notes The foot of smooth astarte is a bright scarlet red or orange because its blood contains hemoglobin—an uncommon trait in mollusks. Beachcombers, however, seldom view the live animal and so rarely see this color. Shells of this species are often found washed up on the beach after a storm.

Wavy Astarte *Astarte undata*

Other Name Waved astarte.

Description The white shells are oval in shape and covered with a light brown periostracum in young specimens (dark brown in adults). Broad concentric ridges cover the exterior of the shells.

Size To 1.5″ (3.8 cm) long.

Habitat In sand, mud, or gravel shores; low intertidal zone to depths of 625′ (191 m).

Range Labrador to Maryland.

Notes The shells of wavy astarte are often found washed ashore on the beach. Its periostracum is often tough enough to remain attached to the shell when it is beached. It is believed that the periostracum is present to help protect the clam from being attacked by predators. The genus name *Astarte* derives from Astartes—a Phoenician goddess of love and fertility.

Adult specimen.

Atlantic Surfclam *Spisula solidissima*

Other Names Surf clam, beach clam, skimmer clam, bar clam, hen clam.

Description The yellowish-white shells are covered with a grayish-yellow periostracum. The shells are roughly triangular in shape and thick-shelled.

Size To 7" (18 cm) long.

Habitat On open exposed sand beaches; low intertidal zone to depths of 140' (42 m).

Range Nova Scotia to South Carolina.

Notes Atlantic surfclam is unlike many other clams because it does not remain in its burrow. Instead it travels along the surface of the sand with a series of "jumps" by using its muscular foot. This large species is also reported to be able to "leap" when it is distressed. Northern moonsnail (p. 73), lobed moonsnail (p. 72), Jonah crab (p. 124), and Forbes' sea star (p. 129) are included in the list of its predators. Atlantic surfclam is also the basis of an important commercial fishery.

Similar Species **Dwarf surfclam** *Mulinia lateralis* is a small species, as its common name suggests, that reaches a length of 0.8" (2 cm) . This species is found in sheltered areas such as shallow tidal estuaries. At times it may form the main course for several species of waterfowl from Maine to Florida and Texas.

Arctic Wedgeclam *Mesodesma arctatum*

Other Name Scientific name formerly written as *M. arctata*.

Description The white wedge-shaped shells are shiny with a yellow periostracum. A hinge is present one third of the distance from hind end and a chondrophore (spoon-shaped projection) is present on the inside of one shell.

Size To 2.25" (5.7 cm) long.

Habitat In sand; low intertidal zone to depths of 39' (12 m).

Range Greenland to Chesapeake Bay.

Notes Shells of Arctic wedgeclam are often found washed up upon the shore. Some shells have a round hole drilled into them, evidence of predation by a snail. Common, white-winged and surf scoters also feed on these small clams.

Atlantic Razor-clam *Siliqua costata*

Other Names Atlantic razor, ribbed pod, fragile razor clam.
Description The shells' exterior is white, covered with a shiny greenish to yellowish-brown periostracum, and the interior is purplish white. The shells are oval in shape, with a strong internal rib and a hinge that is off-center forward.
Size To 2.5" (64 mm) long.
Habitat In sand; low intertidal zone to depths of 240' (73 m).
Range Gulf of St. Lawrence to Cape Hatteras.
Notes The thin, flat shells of Atlantic razor-clam often wash up on shore from deeper waters. Although the shells of this species are elongated, they are easily identified by their hinge placement and shape. Atlantic razor-clam is distinguished from the similar-looking stout tagelus (p. 101) by the presence of a strong rib on the inside of Atlantic razor-clam's shells.

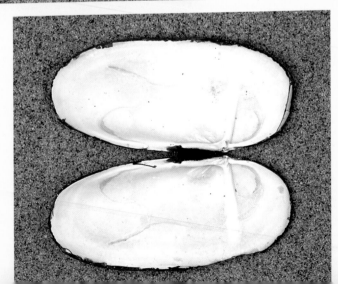

Stout Tagelus *Tagelus plebeius*

Other Names Stout razor clam, little razor, jackknife clam, spit clam.
Description The shells' exterior is white, covered in a thick olive-green to brownish-yellow periostracum, and the interior is white. The elongated shells have a central hinge. The valves are squared off at the anterior end, while the rear end is rounded.
Size To 4" (102 mm) long.
Habitat In muddy sand beaches near marshes; low intertidal zone to depths of 20' (6 m).
Range Cape Cod, Massachusetts to Florida and Texas.
Notes The presence of this common species is sometimes revealed when it squirts water from its burrow when it is disturbed. Stout tagelus burrows 8–20" (20–50 cm) below the surface of its substrate. This clam feeds on small particles of food suspended in the water. The shells of this species are often washed up on the beach after a storm.

The shell interior of stout tagelus is white.

Similar Species Purplish tagelus *T. divisus* is a smaller species that reaches to 1.6" (41 mm) long. This interior of this species is purple, as its common name suggests. The exterior has a chestnut-brown periostracum. This species is found from Cape Cod, Massachusetts to the West Indies and Brazil.

Atlantic Jackknife-clam *Ensis directus*

Other Names Atlantic jackknife, common straight-razor, common razor clam, jackknife clam.

Description The shells' exterior is white and covered in a varnish-like greenish-brown to olive-brown periostracum. The elongated shells are curved moderately and the two ends are squared off abruptly. The hinge is found at the hind end.

Size To 10" (25 cm) long.

Habitat In sand or muddy sand of protected waters; low intertidal zone to shallow subtidal depths.

Range Labrador to Florida.

Notes Atlantic jackknife-clam stands upright in its burrow and may be viewed protruding from its burrow at low tide. At the slightest disturbance, however, it retreats back into its burrow. This species is also capable of swimming for short bursts using jet propulsion. Northern moonsnail (p. 73) is its main predator.

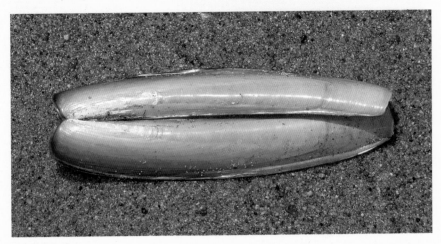

Northern Dwarf-tellin *Tellina agilis*

Other Names Dwarf tellin; formerly classified as *T. tenera*.

Description The shells' exterior is glossy white or yellow to pink with a rounded front end. The surface is sculptured with a series of faint concentric lines.

Size To 0.66" (17 mm) long.

Habitat In sandy bays and shallows; low intertidal zone to shallow subtidal depths.

Range Gulf of St. Lawrence to North Carolina.

Notes Northern dwarf-tellin is the northern representative of several similar tellins that are found in warmer waters to the south. Its siphons are long and, like the macomas', separate. This is unusual: most bivalves have their siphons fused together along their entire length. The delicate shells of this species are normally found on sandy beaches.

Baltic Macoma *Macoma balthica*

Description The oval shells are white but can also be pink, blue, orange, or yellow in color. These shells are thin and chalky, with a front end that is rounded and a hind end that is slightly narrowed.

Size To 1.5" (4 cm) long.

Habitat In areas with mud and sand mixed, mudflats, and eelgrass beds; the mid-intertidal zone to depths of 130' (39 m).

Range Arctic to Georgia.

Notes Baltic macoma is often plentiful in muddy areas. Members of the genus *Macoma* have two separate siphons—one for the water to enter and the other for the water and wastes to leave. The siphons extend from where the clam is buried in order to reach the surface for it to feed, breathe, and expel wastes. The incurrent siphon operates much like a vacuum cleaner, sucking up detritus as it moves across the surface of the mud.

False Angelwing *Petricola pholadiformis*

Other Names American piddock, false angel wing.
Description The exterior of the shells is chalky white, and the front bears approximately 10 scaly radiating ribs. Their thin, elongated shells are cylindrical.
Size To 2" (51 mm) long.
Habitat In mud, clay, or peat; low intertidal zone to shallow subtidal.
Range Gulf of St. Lawrence to Florida.

"Siphon show."

Notes As its name suggests, false angelwing is similar to another bivalve, angelwing *Cyrtopleura costata*—a similar-looking species that is larger in size but found farther south. False angelwing uses its file-like shell surface to burrow in various media. Many individuals are normally found living closely together.

Queen Quahog *Arctica islandica*

Other Names Black clam, ocean clam, mahogany clam.
Description The shells' exterior is white, covered with a yellowish-brown periostracum in young specimens and a dark brown to black periostracum in older individuals. No pallial sinus is present on the inside of its white shell interior. Its round shape is graced with fine concentric growth lines.
Size To 5" (12.7 cm) long.
Habitat In sandy substrates; in water 30–840' (9–265 m) deep.
Range Newfoundland to North Carolina.
Notes Queen quahog is an esteemed food item that forms the basis of a commercial fishery off the mid-Atlantic United States. The shells of this shallow burrower are frequently washed ashore after storms. Its circular shape, lack of purple on the inside of the shell, and very dark periostracum help to aid in its identification. Queen quahog is a very slow growing species that likely lives more than 100 years, although growth after age 20 is exceedingly slow.

Northern Quahog *Mercenaria mercenaria*

Other Names Hard clam, cherrystone clam, bay quahaug, little neck clam, chowder clam; formerly classified as *Venus mercenaria*.

Description The exterior of the oval shells is gray, and the interior is white with bright purple edges near the siphons. The surface is sculpted with a series of faint concentric lines.

Size To 5" (127 mm) long.

Habitat In sand or mud; high to low intertidal zone.

Range Gulf of St. Lawrence to Florida and Texas.

Shell of a juvenile.

Notes Northern quahog is an important species that is harvested commercially. It is known by several common names, depending upon the size. Young quahogs (cherrystones) are the most succulent and so are served on the half-shell. Larger and tougher quahogs (hard-shells or littlenecks) are served steamed or made into chowders. Northern quahog is able to live for weeks after it is harvested since it remains tightly closed when refrigerated out of water. As a result, it is a highly desirable item in the food industry. The shells of juveniles often bear numerous concentric ribs and are often thought to be another species. In times past, the purple-tinged shells of this species were used as a currency (wampum) by native North American peoples.

Similar Species Shells of **false quahog** **Pitar morrhuanus** may also be found on beaches from the Gulf of St. Lawrence to North Carolina. These thin, round shells range from gray to brownish red on the exterior and white without purple staining on the interior. The pillial sinus is moderately deep.

The purple stains of the shell interior identify the species as northern quahog.

Softshell-clam *Mya arenaria*

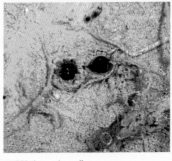

Other Names Softshell, Soft-shelled clam, long neck clam, long-necked clam, steamer, nanny nose.

Description The white shells are covered with a gray to yellowish periostracum. The shells are thin and relatively soft, with a large chondrophore (spoon-shaped projection) at the hinge of the left shell.

Size To 5.5" (14 cm) long.

Habitat In sand, mud, or clay; mid-intertidal zone to depths of 240' (73 m).

Range Labrador to North Carolina.

"Siphon show."

Notes Softshell-clam is a favorite species that is commonly gathered throughout its range. This delectable clam often announces its presence by squirting water into the air just as an unsuspecting seashore visitor walks by. This occurs as the clam withdraws its siphons from the surface to retreat to a lower, safer location. It burrows in mud and sand in a unique way. Water is ejected below the clam, pushing sand out of the way and enabling the clam to move to a deeper location. This slow method of

burrowing is more effective in sand than in mud. This clam also has a special sack off the stomach that holds a food reserve. Its enemies include several diving ducks, raccoons, rays, as well as humans. If you plan to harvest this clam, be sure to check for current limits, restrictions, and closures. This species was accidentally introduced to California in 1865 or 1870.

A large chondrophore helps to identify the shell of this species.

Truncated Softshell-clam *Mya truncata*

Other Names Truncate soft shell clam, truncated mya, blunt softshell clam, mud gaper, blunt gaper.

Description The dull white shells are covered by a yellowish-brown periostracum. The shells are heavy with a wide flaring gap, a round anterior end, and a truncated posterior end.

Size To 3" (7.5 m) long.

Habitat In mud or clay; low intertidal zone to depths of 300' (990 m).

Range Arctic to Massachusetts.

Notes The enormous siphons of truncated softshell-clam are too large to be completely retracted into the shells of the live animal. This species is an important food source for the walrus in northern waters. Its shells are easily identified by the posterior end, which appears to be chopped off.

Arctic Hiatella *Hiatella arctica*

Other Names Arctic saxicave, rock borer, red-nosed clam.

Description The white shells are covered with a gray periostracum. The chalky shells are oblong, oval, or twisted in shape, and the dorsal and ventral margins are roughly parallel. The beaks lie one third from the anterior end.

Size To 3" (7.6 cm) long.

Habitat In old bore holes, crevices, and similar sites; low intertidal zone to depths of 600' (183 m).

Range Arctic to the West Indies.

Notes The shape of this bivalve's shells varies greatly, as it takes on the contour of its surroundings. This species thrives in cold water and as a result is found in deep water in the southern portion of its range. Arctic hiatella is also found along the Pacific coast from the Arctic to Panama as well as in Europe.

Common Shipworm *Teredo navalis*

Other Name Shipworm.

Description The white shells are blade-like at the front end. The worm-like animal has 2 paddle-like appendages at its rear end and a sucker-like foot. The pallet is funnel-shaped and not segmented.

Size The shells are up to 0.25" (6 mm) long and the entire animal to 12" (30 cm) long; burrows may be as long as 24" (60 cm) and up to 0.33" (0.8 cm) in diameter.

Habitat In submerged wood above the substrate; high intertidal zone to depths of 100' (30 m).

Range Arctic to the tropics; worldwide.

Notes Common shipworm has a nasty reputation that has persisted for hundreds of years. This

species bores into wood with great efficiency. As a result most structures today at or in the ocean are made with metal or concrete. It is a bivalve rather than a worm, despite its common name and appearance. It drills into wood and tunnels along the wood's grain—the path of least resistance. Its mantle produces a calcareous lining that covers the inside of the tunnel. Siphons are formed at its posterior, and these extend out from the tunnel to keep water flowing over the gills' filter feeder. Special pallets or plugs are used to seal the opening when the wood is out of water. These pallets enable the common shipworm to continue to live for weeks if the wood remains out of water.

Similar Species **Northern gribble** (p. 115) produces similar burrows; however, its holes are much smaller in diameter.

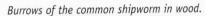

Burrows of the common shipworm in wood.

Great Piddock *Zirfaea crispata*

Other Name Common piddock.

Description The shells' exterior is white, covered in a brown or blackish periostracum (skin-like covering). The shells are oval in shape and gape at both ends. An oblique groove runs across the width of the shell, separating the anterior section with scale-like ribs from the posterior section with a smooth surface. A hard shield-like plate is also present that covers the umbones.

Size To 3.5" (89 mm) long.

Habitat Normally burrows into peat but is also found in clay or soft rock; low inter-tidal zone to depths of 240' (73 m).

Range Labrador to New Jersey.

Notes Great pid-dock is a common bivalve that varies in size depending upon the sub-strate in which it burrows. It is also occasionally found burrowed in water-logged wood. The siphons are fused and form an elongated neck-like shape. This species is also found in Europe.

Gould's Pandora *Pandora gouldiana*

Other Name Rounded pandora.

Description The exterior of the flat shells is white to rust colored. The left shell is convex, and the right is flattened. The shells' upper margins are concave, and the posterior end is blunt.

Size To 1.5" (3.8 cm) long.

Habitat In mud and sand; low intertidal zone to depths of 480' (146 m).

Range Gulf of St. Lawrence to North Carolina.

Notes Shells of Gould's pandora often are found on shore; these typically have the white outer shell layer worn away, which reveals the wonderful pearly layer beneath. At some loca-tions, the live animals can be detected by the presence of maiden hair sea lettuce (p. 149), which marks the location of its siphons in the mud.

Acadian Hermit *Pagurus acadianus*

Arthropods
Phylum Arthropoda

Arthropods are the most widespread group of creatures in the animal kingdom. Arthropoda means "jointed foot," a feature present in all species. All arthropods have an exoskeleton of chitin and a complete digestive tract; growth occurs by molting. Non-marine species include insects, spiders, and mites. Marine arthropods include barnacles, isopods, amphipods, shrimps, and crabs. Many species of arthropods have been and are currently important sources of food for humans, including Atlantic rock crab and American lobster.

Arachnids (Class Arachnida)

Arachnids are eight-legged invertebrates with two body parts: the cephalothorax (prosoma) and abdomen (opisthosoma). Members of this class also have book lungs (modified gills) or tracheae (windpipes) and pedipalps (antennae-like structures), but true antennae are absent. The most common groups in the class Arachnida are spiders, mites, ticks, scorpions, and related organisms.

Red Velvet Mite *Neomolgus littoralis*

Other Names Intertidal mite, red shore mite.
Description Bright scarlet red overall with short dense "hairs" that cover the body; a microscope is needed to see these hair-like structures.
Size To 0.2" (3 mm) in length.
Habitat On rocks and similar objects; high intertidal to splash zone.
Range Nova Scotia and South.
Notes Red velvet mite has 8 legs, like all arachnids—including spiders and ticks. Insects have only 6 legs. This species is often observed scurrying about the spray zone in the heat of the day. This mite has also been observed using its snout-like mouthparts to feed on the fluids of dead flies. Additional studies are needed to determine other foods and the general natural history of this species. The intense red color of this minute creature is best appreciated with a hand lens.

Barnacles (Class Cirripedia)

Barnacles use their cirri or modified legs to sweep through the water like a net to collect tiny planktonic food. Reproduction for this group is complex. Barnacles are hermaphrodytic (both male and female), but they do not release their gametes into the sea. Instead they fertilize another individual internally. When they are ready to reproduce, one adult acts as a male and uncoils its long tubular penis to extend it out through the operculum and search for a receptive neighbor. The second individual must be close enough for its penis to reach, as they are unable to move from their substrate. The penis however, can be uncoiled to reach up to 20 times the length of the barnacle's body. The second barnacle acts as the female and broods the eggs until they hatch as a minute larvae. The larvae swim until they are ready to settle head-down on a suitable surface. A single adult barnacle may release over 10,000 larvae into the water as plankton. There are two types of barnacles: acorn barnacles, in which the plates attach directly to a rock or similar surface, and goose barnacles, which include a stalk.

Northern Rock Barnacle *Semibalanus balanoides*

Other Names Common rock barnacle; formerly classified as *Balanus balanoides*.
Description The grayish white shell is rough with several folds. There is no calcareous base to the shell.
Size To 1" (25 mm) in diameter at base, 0.5" (13 mm) high.
Habitat On rocks; low intertidal zone to shallow subtidal depths.
Range Arctic to Delaware.
Notes Northern rock barnacle is the most common species of barnacle found in the Atlantic Northeast. This species is also found in the Pacific Northwest. Under crowded conditions, the shape of the shells becomes tall and narrow as they grow up rather than out. There is an easy technique to determine whether a barnacle's shell base is calcareous. Locate an empty shell of a barnacle that is still attached to a rock. If the rock beneath the shell is visible, then there is no calcareous base (see photograph).
Similar Species **Rough barnacle *Balanus balanus*** has a rough shell as well as a calcareous base to its shell. It is also found at lower levels from the low intertidal zone to subtidal depths of 544' (165 m).

Ivory Barnacle *Balanus eburneus*

Description The ivory white shell is smooth without folds. Its base is calcareous. The soft tissue often displays purple or yellow stripes.
Size To 1" (25 mm) in diameter at base, 1" (25 mm) high.
Habitat On rocks and pilings in bays and harbors; low intertidal zone to shallow subtidal depths.
Range Maine to South America.
Notes Ivory barnacle is a species of concern to boat owners. It often attaches itself to boats in harbors. It can thrive in salinities near that of fresh water.

Bay Barnacle *Balanus improvisus*

Description The white shell is smooth and flat with a calcareous base. The soft tissue displays pink to purple speckles.
Size To 0.5" (13 mm) in diameter at base, 0.25" (6 mm) high.
Habitat On rocks, pilings, and similar objects including the shells of oysters; low intertidal zone to depths of 120' (37 m).
Range Nova Scotia to Florida and Texas.

Notes Bay barnacle is a small, "flattened" species that is very tolerant of low salinities. Like ivory barnacle, it commonly fouls the hulls of boats.

Note the calcareous base.

Pelagic Goose Barnacle *Lepas anatifera*

Other Names Common goose barnacle.
Description The plates are gray to bluish-gray, and the body varies from orange-brown to purplish-brown, with a brilliant scarlet-orange edge opening. An elongated stalk supports its flat and wedge-shaped body.
Size To 2.75" (7 cm) wide, 6" (15 cm) long.
Habitat Normally found on driftwood; floating in the open ocean.
Range Cosmopolitan.

Notes This gregarious barnacle is a creature of the high seas. The young are attracted to floating objects, which become home to hundreds or thousands of these barnacles. Once the "colonies" have been afloat for some time, they mature and produce their young. To observe this species on shore, one must walk on the beach after a storm to find a stranded float, bottle, or log on which these barnacles have settled.

Shrimps, Crabs, Isopods, Amphipods, and Allies (Class Malacostraca)

Members of this large clan include shrimps, crabs, hermits, lobsters, isopods, amphipods, and similar organisms. Several characteristics are present in all species, including 3 body parts: head with 5 fused segments, thorax with 8 segments, and abdomen with 6 to 7 segments. The head and thorax are fused together and often covered by a carapace, which may have a prominent rostrum (beak-like structure). Two pairs of antennae are also present. The class Malacostraca is the largest group of crustaceans. In general, isopods are flattened dorso-ventrally, while amphipods are flattened laterally.

Isopods (Order Isopoda)

Northern Gribble *Limnoria lignorum*

Other Names Gribble, boring isopod.
Description The body is grayish and slender, with 7 pairs of pereiopods or legs. The dorsal surface of the last segment is smooth.
Size To 0.2" (0.5 cm) long; burrow to 0.6" (2 mm) in diameter.
Habitat On or burrowing into submerged wood; low intertidal zone to shallow subtidal depths.
Range Newfoundland to Rhode Island.
Notes Often referred to as "the termite of the sea," this species causes considerable damage to wooden docks, boats, and similar wooden structures. Numerous tiny holes penetrating wood signify the presence of this species. These worm-like creatures only burrow to a maximum of 0.5" (12 mm) from the surface of the wood. A male and female are normally found in each burrow. Although gribbles ingest wood, their food

is actually a wood-dwelling fungus that inhabits the wood. Under ideal conditions, up to 400 animals have been found to inhabit one square inch of wood.
Similar Species Common shipworm (p. 108) is also often encountered on the same wood surface. The diameter of their holes is much larger—up to 0.33" (0.8 cm).

Burrows of the northern gribble (above) and larger holes of common shipworm (below).

Baltic Isopod *Idotea baltica*

Description The body ranges from green or brown to reddish in a wide variety of patterns. Its thorax is comprised of seven segments each with a pair of pereiopods or legs. The tail segment of the abdomen is squared off with a pointed tip in the middle.

Size To 1" (25 mm) long.
Habitat On rocks, algae, and eelgrass; low intertidal zone to shallow subtidal depths.
Range Gulf of St. Lawrence to North Carolina.
Notes Baltic isopod is an abundant species that feeds on various vegetation including the leaves of eelgrass (p. 175) and northern rockweed (p. 160). Pairs are often observed in early summer copulating and swimming together, with the male beneath the larger, clinging female. This species may also be observed swarming at night. It is the largest isopod found in the Northeast. The tailpiece of the Baltic isopod is distinctive and its best identifying characteristic.

Sharp-tailed Isopod *Idotea phosphorea*

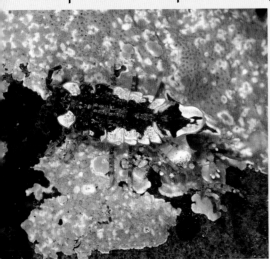

Other Name Isopod.
Description This species' colors are variable, and they are often patterned with banding or mottling in white, gray, brown, red, yellow, or greenish. The tailpiece is arrowhead-shaped.
Size To 0.5" (13 mm) long.
Habitat On rocky shorelines and in tidepools; low intertidal zone to shallow subtidal depths.
Range Gulf of St. Lawrence to Cape Cod.
Notes Sharp-tailed isopod dines on dead vegetation, including eelgrass leaves and the associated diatoms and detritus. It also plays an important role in the shredding of eelgrass, which accelerates the breakdown process of the tough eelgrass leaves and thus provides food for other organisms.

Amphipods (Order Amphipoda)

Tide-pool Scud *Gammarus oceanicus*

Other Names Scud, sideswimmer.
Description The overall color
ranges from red or orange to
green or brown. Two pairs of
equally long antennae are present, and the tailpiece is longer
than wide and has a noticeable
cleft in the center. Its eyes are
kidney shaped.
Size To 1" (25 mm) long.
Habitat In tidepools, under rocks
and seaweeds; mid-intertidal
zone to depths of 100' (30 m).
Range Arctic to Chesapeake Bay.

Notes Tide-pool scud is one of the more common amphipods found in the intertidal
world. A scud moves about on its side with swimming or crawling actions and as a
result is often called a sideswimmer. Because several similar-looking species may be
encountered in the Northeast, this large species requires a microscope and key to
confirm its identification. Tide-pool scud feeds on various invertebrates, including
worms and crustaceans. It is also found in Europe.

Pink Beach Hopper *Maera danae*

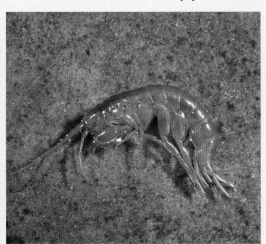

Other Name Formerly classified as
Leptothoe danae.
Description This species' overall
color is pink, and its eyes are rather
small. There are two sets of antennae—the first of which is longer and
has an accessory flagellum attached.
The second set is covered with many
hair-like setae. The tailpiece is
deeply lobed with many setae.
Size To 0.75" (18 mm) long.
Habitat On rocky and muddy shorelines; low intertidal zone to depths
of 328' (100 m).
Range Gulf of St. Lawrence to Cape
Cod, Massachusetts.
Notes Pink beach hopper is one of
the more visible amphipods found on intertidal shores. Females are ovigerous, car-
rying their eggs on their body from March to May along the East Coast. This colorful amphipod is also found along the Pacific Coast of North America from Alaska to
California.

Skeleton Shrimp *Caprella* spp. & *Aeginina* spp.

Description Body tan to reddish or colorless with a slender thorax and legs.
Size To 2.1" (54 mm) long.
Habitat On seaweed, rocks, sponges, and hydroids; low intertidal zone to depths of 7,450' (2,271 m).
Range Arctic to North Carolina.
Notes Skeleton shrimp are sometimes referred to as the "praying mantises of the sea" because they sit upright and their front legs are positioned much like that of the praying mantis. Their pigmentation and slow movements make them well camouflaged in their surroundings. Skeleton shrimp move about inchworm fashion, first by first grasping a hold with their front legs and then moving their back legs. After mating, a female places her eggs in a brood pouch located on the middle of her body. The young hatch directly into miniature adults and leave the safety of her brood pouch. One species of skeleton shrimp is truly amazing because it can be found from intertidal sites to deep sea locations as far down as 1.4 miles (2.3 km).

Shrimp & Crabs (Order Decopoda)

Sevenspine Bay Shrimp *Crangon septemspinosa*

Other Names Sand shrimp, bay shrimp; scientific name also written as *C. septemspinosus*.
Description The coloration varies from transparent to gray or buff overall. It has a short rostrum (beak-like structure), one tooth on the midline of the carapace, and the moveable portion of its claw is bent backward. The body is flattened top to bottom.
Size To 2.75" (70 mm) long.
Habitat On sandy shores end eelgrass beds; low intertidal zone to depths of 300' (91 m).
Range Arctic to Florida.
Notes This common shrimp is easy to miss, as it has excellent cryptic coloration. It settles into the sand, burying itself within seconds. The eyes are positioned on the top of its head, so it is able to view potential predators when buried in the sand.

This species is easy to identify: it has a short rostrum and claws on the first pair of walking legs—unlike most shrimp species.

American Lobster *Homarus americanus*

Other Names Northern lobster, lobster.
Description The shrimp-shaped body is dark green with orange edges; 2 large pincers (claws) are prominent.
Size To 34" (86 cm) long, but much smaller intertidally.
Habitat On rocky and muddy shorelines in quiet bays and the open ocean; low intertidal zone to the edge of the Continental Shelf.
Range Labrador to Virginia.

Notes American lobster is a distinctive, even unmistakable species. Smaller individuals are sometimes found in the intertidal zone, whereas the largest individuals make the deep waters near the Continental Slope their home. They have two large claws: a heavy crusher claw and a smaller cutter claw. The crusher claw is used to open the shells of snails, bivalves, crabs, and even other lobsters: lobsters are highly cannibalistic. The smaller claw is for dining on its food, which also includes plant material and carrion. Adults reach maturity at about 5 years and may live for over 100 years, growing to weigh 60 pounds (27 kg). Few ever reach near this age or size today. It is estimated that 90% of all lobsters living in New England will be captured as food.

Atlantic Horseshoe Crab *Limulus polyphemus*

Other Names Horseshoe crab, king crab.
Description A greenish-tan to brown carapace (upper shell) covers much of the body, and a long unjointed spike-like tail (telson) brings up the rear.
Size To 12" (30 cm) wide, 24" (61 cm) long.
Habitat On sand or mud shorelines; low intertidal zone to depths of 75' (23 m).

Range Gulf of Maine to the Yucatan peninsula.
Notes Atlantic horseshoe crab is often referred to as a "living fossil" because the fossil record shows that very similar species existed as far back as 250 million years ago. This primitive-looking creature is not a true crab but rather it is actually more closely related to the spider. True crabs have 2 pairs of antennae, a pair of mandibles, a pair of claws, and 4 pairs of legs. Horseshoe crabs do not have antennae or mandibles but do have 5 pairs of legs, including 4 pairs with pincers. They use the small pincers in front for maneuvering food that includes worms, clams, and other invertebrates. Horseshoe crabs weigh up to 10 lbs (4.5 kg) and take 9–10 years to reach maturity; they can live to be 17 years old.

Atlantic Mole Crab *Emerita talpoida*

Other Name Atlantic sand crab.
Description The grayish tan body is egg-shaped with a spear-shaped tail and two pairs of antennae, the second pair of which is long and feathery (normally tucked away under the carapace).
Size To 0.75" (19 mm) wide, 1" (25 mm) long.
Habitat On wave-swept sandy beaches; high to low intertidal zones.
Range Cape Cod to Texas.
Notes Atlantic mole crabs favor warm waters and as a result are only found as far north as Cape Cod. This species is not a true crab and does not bite. It constantly burrows in the sand during the summer months and favors the sand at the very edge of the waves. The females reach up to 1" in length, while males only reach half that size. This species is commonly used as bait by fishermen within its range farther south.

Carapace.

Acadian Hermit *Pagurus acadianus*

Other Name Acadian hermit crab.
Description The legs are reddish-brown to orange with a white base overall, and the pincers are white with a reddish-orange stripe down the middle. The right first walking leg is enlarged.
Size To 1" (25 mm) wide, 1.25" (32 mm) long.
Habitat In tidepools; low intertidal zone to depths of 1,600' (488 m).
Range Labrador to Chesapeake Bay.
Notes Acadian hermits live in the shells of various snails, including those of common periwinkle (p. 68). As they grow, they exchange these shells for larger ones. Hermits remain inside the shell except to move into a larger shell or to mate. The shell protects the soft unprotected parts of the crab and provides a place where the crab can draw in its appendages in times of danger. It also provides protection for the female's eggs. The bright red colors of this species often attract the viewer's attention in a tidepool, and these colors help to identify this species.

Longwrist Hermit *Pagurus longicarpus*

Other Name Long-clawed hermit.
Description This species is gray to greenish-gray overall and shows a tan stripe with white edge down middle of pincers. The right pincer is much longer than the left; and the "hand" is 3 times longer than it is wide.
Size To 0.5" (13 mm) long, 0.4" (10 mm) wide.
Habitat On rock, sand, or mud shores in protected waters; low intertidal zone to depths of 150' (45 m).

Range Nova Scotia to Texas.
Notes This small hermit crab is the most common hermit along the entire Atlantic coastline. It uses a variety of snail shells as its home, including those of smooth periwinkle (p. 66), rough periwinkle (p. 67), eastern mud snail (p. 81), and Atlantic oyster drill (p. 74). This hermit favors the quiet waters of bays and similar locations. The claws of this species are noticeably long and narrow.

121

Atlantic Hairy Hermit *Pagurus arcuatus*

Other Name Hairy hermit.
Description The body is brown overall and covered with many long bristles. The right pincer is large and covered with round projections.
Size To 1" (25 mm) wide, 1.25" (32 mm) long.
Habitat On rocky shores and tidepools; low intertidal zone to depths of 900' (274 m).
Range Arctic to Long Island Sound.
Notes Small Atlantic hairy hermits are often found living in tidepools. As they grow larger, they move to deeper waters, where they use larger shells such as those of Stimpson's whelk (p. 77) or waved whelk (p. 77). The number of hairs varies greatly in this species.

Atlantic Lyre Crab *Hyas araneus*

Other Names Toad crab, great spider crab.
Description The olive to reddish carapace is violin-shaped. The long, slender legs are banded in orange and red, and its pincers are small.
Size To 2.5" (64 mm) wide, 3.75" (95 mm) long.
Habitat On rocks and in tidepools; low intertidal zone to depths of 170' (52 m).
Range Arctic to Rhode Island.
Notes Atlantic lyre crab is well known for its ability to camouflage itself with algae and various other organisms that it attaches to its shell. Feeding on various algae and polychaetes (annelid worms), this slow-moving crab makes its home in areas with soft substrates.

Similar Species Arctic lyre crab *Hyas coarctatus* is a smaller species that prefers hard substrates. Its carapace is violin-shaped but has a crest-like process on the margin behind the tooth. This species is found from the Arctic to Cape Hatteras.

Atlantic Rock Crab *Cancer irroratus*

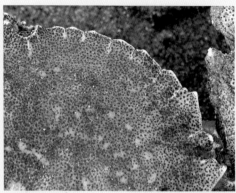

Other Name Rock crab.
Description The yellowish dorsal side is heavily spotted with reddish to purplish-brown. Its fan-shaped carapace is smooth and has 3 teeth between the eyes. There are 9 smooth teeth to the side of each eye socket.
Size To 5.25" (133 mm) wide, 3.5" (89 mm) long.
Habitat On rock, sand gravel shores, and tidepools; low intertidal zone to depths of 2,600' (780 m).
Range Labrador to South Carolina.

Shell detail.

Notes Atlantic rock crab is a predator that feeds on a wide range of creatures, including worms, snails, bivalves, and dead fish. It in turn is preyed upon by fish and birds, including gulls, ducks, and herons. It is also the basis of a commercial fishery. The sex of a crab can be determined by looking at its abdomen, which curls around its underside from behind. A narrow abdomen indicates a male and a wide abdomen a female. Juvenile Atlantic rock crabs may be found in a wide range of colors, including white and blue. This crab is easily confused with the

Jonah crab (p. 124), but a close look at the teeth to the side of the eye (see photograph) will help to distinguish these two species.

Juvenile.

Jonah Crab *Cancer borealis*

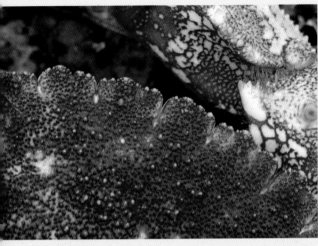

Shell detail.

Other Name Northern crab.
Description The brick red dorsal side is highlighted with purplish spots. Its fan-shaped carapace is granular, with 3 teeth between the eyes. Nine jagged teeth are located to the side of each eye socket.
Size To 6.25" (16 cm) wide; 4" (10 cm) long.

Habitat On rock shores and tidepools; low intertidal zone to depths of 2,620' (799 m).
Range Nova Scotia to Florida.
Notes Jonah crab mates in late summer and, as in all crabs, the female carries her eggs attached to the abdomen. In early summer these eggs hatch, and the young begin their lives as pelagic or free-swimming larvae. These tiny shrimp-like larvae pass through a total of five stages called zoea. The next and last stage, called the megalops, resembles a miniature crab with a shrimp-like tail. Although this crab is found as far south as Florida, it is much more common in the northern parts of its range.

European Green Crab *Carcinus maenas*

Other Names
Green crab,
European shore
crab.

Description
The fan-shaped
shell is green
mottled with
yellow and
black spots.
There are 3
teeth between
the eye sockets
and 5 large
teeth to the
side of each eye
socket.

Size To 3.1" (8
cm) wide; 2.8"
(7 cm) long.

Habitat On
rocks or mud-

flats of sheltered bays and estuaries and in tidepools; low intertidal zone to depths of
20' (6 m).

Range Nova Scotia to New Jersey.

Notes European green crab is an introduced species from Europe that has become
well established in the Atlantic Northeast. Its recent invasions include Australia,
Tasmania, South Africa, Japan, Brazil, and both coasts of North America. It is capable
of surviving exposure to the air for at least 10 days and is tolerant of short expo-
sures to temperatures as low as 0° C (32° F) and as high as 33° C (91° F). This is
an aggressive species, and there are concerns about its negative impacts on native
species. European green crab is just one example of the many species that have been
introduced into areas where they did not occur naturally.

Similar Species
Say mud crab
Dyspanopeus sayi
is a native spe-
cies that may also
be encountered in
a muddy habitat;
it has equal-sized
pincers that show a
black-colored finger.

*Juvenile European
green crab.*

125

Lady Crab *Ovalipes ocellatus*

Other Names Calico crab, ocellated crab.
Description The fan-shaped carapace is yellowish gray with reddish-purple spots scattered in a ring. Its hindmost legs are paddle-shaped.
Size To 3.1" (79 mm) wide, 2.5" (64 mm) long.
Habitat On sand, rock, or mud shores; low intertidal zone to depths of 130' (40 m).
Range Prince Edward Island to South Carolina.
Notes Lady crab is an aggressive species that buries itself completely in sand. Care is required

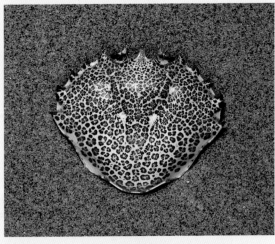

in handling, it as it can deliver a nasty pinch. Its paddle-shaped hind legs indicate that it is a member of the family of swimming crabs (Portunidae). This species is more common in warmer waters south of Cape Cod. As with most true crabs, the empty shells of this species may be found on shore after they are molted.

Asian Shore Crab *Hemigrapsus sanguineus*

Other Names Japanese shore crab, western Pacific shore crab, Pacific crab.
Description The carapace is square-shaped, with colors ranging from greenish to orange-brown or red with red spots on the claws. Three spines are present on each side of the carapace.
Size To 1.7" (42 mm) wide.
Habitat On rocky shorelines; high intertidal zone to shallow subtidal depths.
Range Maine to North Carolina.
Notes Asian shore crab is a small, fast, and secretive invader to our shores. It was first discovered in New Jersey in 1988, and since then it has spread along our shores in both directions. It is native to the Western Pacific Ocean, from Russia to Japan. It was likely introduced through the release of water from the ballast of a ship. This species is capable of producing 50,000 eggs per clutch and may have 3–4 clutches per breeding season.

Atlantic Sand Fiddler *Uca pugilator*

Other Names Sand fiddler, calico-backed fiddler.

Description The carapace is light blue to grayish-blue with a purplish patch on the front section and an "H"-shaped depression positioned centrally. The distance between the eyes is less than a third of the width of the carapace. The surface of large pincer's inner palm is smooth.

Size To 1.5" (38 mm) wide, 1" (25 mm) long.

Habitat On protected sand and sandy-mud beaches; high intertidal zone.

Range Cape Cod, Massachusetts to Florida.

Notes Male fiddlers use their large yellow claw to display visually to females in an elaborate waving motion. They also produce sound signals by vibrating and stamping their walking legs. Together these signals draw females to follow the male into his burrow to mate. At many sites where fiddler crabs are present, more than one species may reside. At such sites the population of fiddlers may reached as many as 45 individuals per square yard (54 per square meter).

Atlantic Marsh Fiddler *Uca pugnax*

Other Names Mud fiddler, calling crab.

Description The carapace is dark olive to nearly black above and the large pincer is yellowish-brown. The distance between the eyes is less than a third of the width of the carapace. The large pincer has an oblique ridge on the inner surface of the hand.

Size To .9" (22 mm) wide, .6" (16 mm) long.

Habitat On protected mud and sandy-mud beaches; high intertidal zone.

Range Cape Cod, Massachusetts to Florida.

Notes The Atlantic marsh fiddler is the most common of the fiddlers found in the Northeast. It makes its burrows in muddy areas

with a high salinity. The males can be either right- or left-clawed. If a male fiddler should loose its large pincer, the other will grow to become the large pincer, and a new smaller one will grow to replace the one lost. Fiddlers are only active in temperatures of 59°F and higher. As a result, they are not active during the colder times of the year.

Female Atlantic marsh fiddler.

Similar Species Redjointed fiddler *Uca minax* is another species that may be encountered as far north as Cape Cod. This species can be identified with the presence of red joints on its large claw.

127

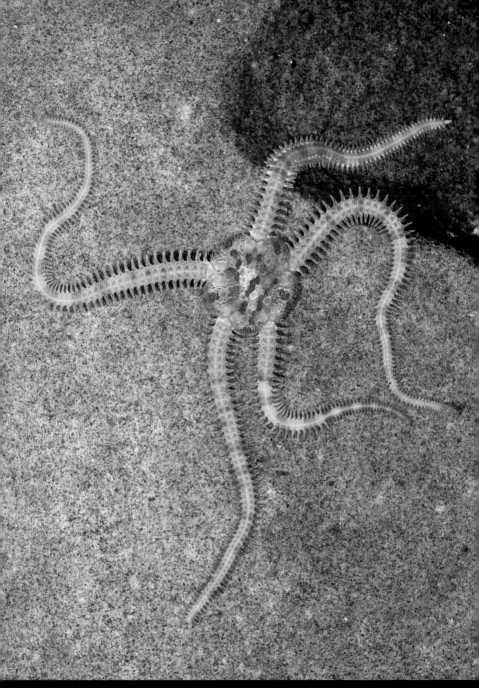

Daisy Brittle Star *Ophiopholis aculeata*

SPINY-SKINNED ANIMALS

The echinoderms (spiny-skinned animals) have ossicles (plates) that make up an internal skeleton that is located below an outer skin layer. The size of the ossicles varies from large and conspicuous types as found in most species (e.g., sea urchins), to inconspicuous (e.g., sea cucumbers). All echinoderms are radially symmetrical with a water vascular system that is made up of a network of radial canals used for both locomotion and respiration. There are approximately 7,000 species in this phylum.

Sea Stars (Class Asteroidea)

Most sea stars (formerly starfish) have 5 distinct rays or arms, but this number is variable. Small pedicellariae (pinching structures) and tube feet are found on the underside of each ray. Tube feet are responsible for movement, and suckers are normally present at the tips. Animals in this group have truly remarkable powers of regeneration. Entire limbs can be regenerated, and in some species, whole sea stars can be regenerated from a single ray with a portion of the central disk or body. It is estimated that there are about 1,500 living species worldwide. The radius of a sea star is measured from the tip of the ray to the center of the disk.

Forbes' Sea Star *Asterias forbesi*

Other Names Common sea star, Forbes' common sea star.

Description The overall color varies from tan or olive to red, purple, or green, and the madreporite or sieve plate is bright orange. Its spines are scattered and do not form any pattern.

Size Radius to 5.1" (13 cm).

Habitat On rocks, sand, or gravel; low intertidal zone to depths of 160' (49 m).

Range Prince Edward Island to Texas.

Notes Forbes' sea star is a predator of several bivalves, including eastern oyster (p. 96) and northern quahog (p. 105). This sea star uses its tube feet to pry open the shells of bivalves and releases a muscle relaxant to help it open the shells. If the shells are pried opened as little as 1/250" (0.1 mm), it can evert its stomach to insert it between the valves to feast upon the meat inside the clam. This is only possible on small clams, as large clams have stronger muscles and keep their shells closed when attacked. Larger clams can be attacked, but they require the combined forces of several sea stars to pry open. Forbes' sea star has been known to hybridize with northern sea star (p. 130) to produce hybrids that appear stunted and exhibit characteristics of both species.

Northern Sea Star *Asterias rubens*

Other Names
Purple sea star;
formerly *A. vulgaris*.

Description
This species'
colors are highly
variable, often
having a hint of
fluorescence and
a pale yellow
sieve plate. Five
rays or arms are
present, each
with 4 rows
of tube feet.
Normally a row of
spines is present
down the center
of each tapered
arm.

Size Radius to 8" (20 cm).

Habitat On rocks, gravel, or in tidepools; high intertidal zone to depths of 1,145' (349 m).

Range Labrador to Cape Hatteras.

Notes Northern sea star is a member of the genus *Asterias*, all of which harbor 4 rows of tube or sucker feet; most sea stars have only 2. This beautiful species can be found in a wide range of colors including rose, pink, orange, green, bluish, tan, gray, and creamy-white. It is also often present in large numbers where there is an abundance of food, particularly mussels, oysters, clams, barnacles, and urchins.

Similar Species Green slender sea star *Leptasterias littoralis* has 6 narrow rays that only reach 1.25" (32 mm) in radius. This greenish species has 2 rows of tube feet and can be found from the Arctic to Maine. The female possesses a brood pouch near her mouth in which she carries her eggs.

Slender-armed sea star *Leptasterias tenera* may also be encountered in colors that range from light purple to pink. A white madreporite (sieve plate) is also present. There are 2 rows of tube feet and normally a total of 5 slender arms. Its upper surface is rough, with spines placed in irregular rows. It may be encountered from Nova Scotia to Cape Hatteras.

Juvenile northern sea stars.

Atlantic Blood Star *Henricia sanguinolenta*

Other Name Blood star.
Description The color is usually red or orange but also purple or yellowish on the dorsal side and yellowish or white beneath. Each of its 5 slender arms has 2 rows of tube feet positioned in grooves.
Size Radius to 4" (102 cm).
Habitat On rocky bottoms and in tidepools; low intertidal zone to depths of 660' (200 m).
Range Arctic to Cape Hatteras.
Notes Atlantic blood star is a striking species that feeds on sponges as well as plankton and detritus suspended in the water. Females brood their eggs, which develop into miniature sea stars without a free-swimming larval

stage. This beautiful species is also found in Europe.

Northern Sun Star *Solaster endeca*

Other Names Smooth sun star, purple sun star.
Description The orange, pink, red, or purple exterior appears smooth and a yellow sieve plate is present. This species has 7–14 arms.
Size Radius to 8" (20 cm).
Habitat On rocky bottoms; low intertidal zone to depths of 1,080' (329 m).
Range Arctic to Cape Cod, Massachusetts.

Notes Northern sun star feeds on sea cucumbers, sea stars, molluscs, and sea urchins. Although this species appears to be smooth, its surface is actually comprised of tiny bristles that cover small stump-like structures called pseudopaxillae. This sea star inhabits deeper waters in the southern portion of its range.

Brittle Stars (Class Ophiuroidea)

Brittle stars resemble true sea stars, but have long, flexible arms and a central, armored, disk-shaped body that is clearly separated from the rays or arms. The pedicellariae (pinching structures) and tube feet are absent on the underside of brittle stars. Brittle stars move by wriggling their rays rather than crawling on hundreds of tube feet like sea stars. Globally there are over 1,600 species of brittle stars and basket stars.

Dwarf Brittle Star *Amphipholis squamata*

Other Names Small brittle star, serpent star, holdfast brittle star, brooding brittle star; formerly classified as *Axiognathus squamata*, *Amphiura squamata*.
Description The dorsal side is grey, tan, or orange overall with a white spot near the base of each arm. Its round disk does not bulge.
Size The disk can reach 0.1" (5 mm) across. The arms are 3 to 4 times the diameter of the central disk.
Habitat Among rock, sand, and loose gravel and in tidepools; high intertidal zone to water 2716' (828 m) deep.
Range Arctic to Florida.
Notes This small brittle star is very mobile and can often be found in tidepools. It

broods its young, which emerge from brood pouches as miniature adults. Its diet consists primarily of diatoms and detritus. The dwarf brittle star is capable of producing bioluminescence. Cells at the base of the spines can be stimulated chemically in the laboratory setting to emit a glowing yellow-green luminescence. The significance of this ability is unknown at present.

Daisy Brittle Star *Ophiopholis aculeata*

Other Names Serpent star, painted brittlestar.

Description This species exhibits a wide range of colors and patterns. The central disk has a scalloped shape with bulges between the arms.

Size The disk can reach 0.9" (22 mm) across, and the arms can reach 3.5 to 4 times the diameter of the central disk.

Habitat Under stones or rocks in algal holdfasts and rocky shores; the low intertidal zone to water 5435' (1657 m) deep.

Range Arctic to Long Island Sound.

Notes This common species, whose common name comes from the flower-like shape of its disk, is more abundant in the northern part of its range. Like other brittle stars, it feeds by scraping off minute organisms from rock with specialized tube feet. The food then enters the stomach, which takes up most of the body cavity. Unlike the sea star, the brittle star cannot extrude its stomach to feed. Strangely enough, there is no intestine or anus; instead food is absorbed along the alimentary canal and wastes go back out the mouth.

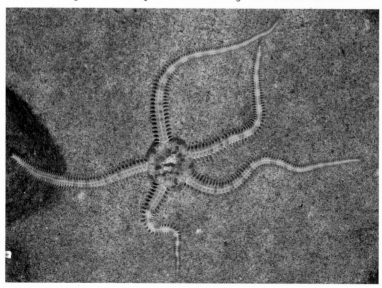

Sea Cucumbers (Class Holothuroidea)

Sea cucumbers are elongated echinoderms that lie on their sides and have an extended groove along the sides of their entire body. There are approximately 1,100 species worldwide, and most species have separate sexes. Reproduction normally occurs with external fertilization of eggs that develop into pelagic larvae, but there are a few species that brood their young. Most species live from 5 to 10 years. Globally some species of sea cucumbers are commercially harvested for food.

Synaptas *Leptosynapta* spp.

Description The elongated body is transparent with a white, yellowish, or pink color overall. No tube feet are present, but 12 pinnate (feather-like) tentacles are found at the front end.
Size To 12" (30 cm) long.
Habitat In muddy sand or under stones; low intertidal zone to shallow subtidal depths.
Range Along the entire coast.
Notes Synaptas are easily misidentified as worms. Indeed, their elongated bodies do not resemble any "normal" members of the sea cucumber clan. To complicate matters further, they are not likely to extend their tentacles while being handled. They feed much like other sea cucumbers, by bringing food to their mouth, one tentacle at a time. A wide variety of small marine life provides food for this group.

Young adult synaptas have been observed swimming at the water's surface in the darkness of late-summer nights. The reason for this behavior is unknown.

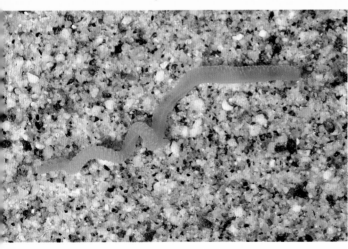

Synapta with tentacles retracted.

Orange-footed Sea Cucumber
Cucumaria frondosa

Other Name Orange-footed cucumber.
Description The reddish-brown to purple body is graced with 10 orange tentacles. Its overall appearance suggests that of a cucumber. Juveniles are often lighter in coloration, from translucent to brown. The tube feet are placed in 5 bands along its body.
Size To 19" (48 cm) long, 5" (12.7 cm) wide, but only half that size in intertidal situations.
Habitat On rocky shorelines; low intertidal zone to depths of 1,208' (368 m).
Range Arctic to Cape Cod.

Notes Orange-footed sea cucumber, the largest sea cucumber present in the Atlantic Northeast, often anchors itself in rock crevices. This species uses its tentacles, which are covered with a sticky mucous, to gather food suspended in the water. Once it has gathered enough food it brings it to the mouth, one tentacle at a time, scraping it off to make a meal. These tentacles are actually modified tube feet that are retractable, just as their tube feet are.

Many sea cucumbers are able to expel their inner organs from their rear end. This action is a seasonal event and thought to foil the attack of a predator—leaving them with a pile of viscera rather than the entire animal. The sea cucumber is then able to regenerate the missing organs over time—one of the abilities of several echinoderms. American lobster is one of this species' predators.

Juvenile.

135

Sea Urchins & Sand Dollars (Class Echinoidea)

Sea urchins and sand dollars feed with the help of a jaw-like apparatus known as Aristotle's lantern, a unique arrangement of parts including teeth. Members of this group have ossicles (plates) that overlap and are fused together into a globular or disk-shaped test (skeleton). Their spines and tube feet are used in locomotion, burrowing, and food gathering. Sea urchins and sand dollars have five sets of pores arranged in a petal pattern that is visible on the outer test. Sea water enters through these pores into an internal water-vascular system, which facilitates locomotion. There are over 800 different species of sea urchins and sand dollars worldwide.

Green Sea Urchin
Strongylocentrotus droebachiensis

Other Name Sea egg.
Description The greenish-brown test (round skeleton) is protected with light-green spines. The spines are less than a third the diameter of the test.
Size To 3.25" (83 mm) in diameter.
Habitat On rocky shorelines and kelp beds; low intertidal zone to depths of 3,795' (1,157 m).
Range Arctic to New Jersey.
Notes Green sea urchin is an "herbivore" well known for its ability to reach high population levels and move en masse into new areas via "urchin fronts." Researchers believe that the long-lived planktonic larvae of the green sea urchin are capable of travelling up to 1,000 km before they settle. This would help them greatly in relocating to areas with a plentiful food sources and to locations where disease has eliminated local populations.

   Although algae are its favorite food, this species will also feed on mussels, sponges, carrion, and other species; underwater "urchin barrens" are created when

large numbers of urchins deplete food stocks. Their enemies include gulls, large sea stars, fishes, lobsters, and of course humans. Green sea urchin is commercially harvested in the Atlantic Northeast and commercially farmed in Europe. This fishery has increased dramatically since the mid 1980s. Also present in the Pacific Northwest, the species has one of the longest scientific names in the animal kingdom, *Strongylocentrotus droebachiensis*.

Common Sand Dollar *Echinarachnius parma*

Other Name Sand dollar.
Description The test is reddish-brown to purple on the dorsal side and lighter below. A series of very short spines cover the disk-shaped test. The upper surface has a pattern of 5 petal-like loops.
Size To 3.1" (79 mm) in diameter.
Habitat On sandy shores; low intertidal zone to depths of 5,280' (1,613 m).
Range Labrador to Maryland.
Notes The spines on the dorsal side of sand dollars are covered with fine, hair-like cilia. These cilia, in combination with a mucous coating, move food around to the oral side, where it travels in food

grooves to the mouth opening on the underside. Enemies of common sand dollar include sea stars and a few bottom-feeding fishes. It is likely that many predators pass over sand dollars because of their hard test; they also offer little in the way of nourishment. The white tests often found on the beach are the empty skeletons of this species.

Sand dollar pea crab *Dissodactylus mellitae* is a tiny species (less than 0.25" [6 mm] wide) that lives on live common sand dollars as well as on their empty tests. This symbiotic crab is also found on two additional species of sand dollars farther south.

Test of a dead common sand dollar.

Sea Pork *Aplidium* sp.

TUNICATES

Phylum Chordata, Class Ascidiacae

Tunicates, also called sea squirts or ascidians, are members of the phylum Chordata, because their larvae posses a notochord. Formerly included in the phylum Urochordata, members of this group are non-vertebrate cordates. Tunicates may be solitary or colonial in nature.

Colonial tunicates may be either social, in which several individual zooids are joined at the base by a common connection, or compound, in which the zooids are fused and have a common tunic and excurrent siphon. Tunicates are shaped like a sac called a tunic, hence the name tunicate. Solitary species are oval, elongated, or irregular in shape, and individuals are usually attached directly to the substrate by the side or base. All sea squirts have two siphons, an incurrent siphon to obtain water for food and for respiration and an excurrent siphon to expel water and non-food particles. One unique feature of tunicates is the heart, which reverses its beating every few minutes to change the direction in the flow of blood. The purpose of this system is currently unknown. It is truly remarkable that the simple-looking tunicates are one of the most advanced groups of organisms found in the intertidal zone. Tunicates are distantly related to fishes, whales, and humans.

Orange Sea Grape Tunicate *Molgula citrina*

Description The orange gonads (reproductive organs) are visible through the transparent greenish to olive tunic. The tunic is not covered with particles or debris. Its short siphons are widely separated.
Size To 0.7" (18 mm) high.
Habitat On rocks; low intertidal zone to shallow subtidal depths.
Range Gulf of St. Lawrence to Rhode Island.
Notes The orange sea grape tunicate varies greatly in shape from rather flattened to nearly round. The tadpole-shaped young are brooded inside the tunic of the adults. This method of reproduction is not common in sea squirts. The orange sea grape tunicate is also found naturally in Europe from the Arctic to France. Several similar species are also found along the Atlantic coast. Positive identification may require dissection.
Similar Species **Common sea grape tunicate M. manhattennis** is normally hairy and muddy with an overall gray to greenish coloration. It may be observed from the Bay of Fundy, Nova Scotia, to the Gulf of Mexico but is more common south of Cape Cod. This species is often found at polluted sites.

Orange Sheath Tunicate *Botrylloides violaceus*

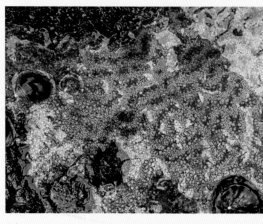

Other Names Violet tunicate; also classified as *B. violaceous*.
Description This species may be one of many bright colors, with orange, red, yellow, and purple being the most common. The zooids are arranged in irregular oval patterns with dark lines or grooves between the zooid groups.
Size Colony to 6" (15 cm) and greater.
Habitat On rocks, floats, kelp, and various other organisms; low intertidal zone to shallow subtidal waters.
Range Prince Edward Island to Virginia.
Notes The orange sheath tunicate likely originates from Japan. It is now present in most temperate harbors and marinas throughout the world. This spread is believed to be a result of worldwide warming of the oceans, which has probably permitted this species to survive in areas where it was not able to live previously. Predators of the orange sheath tunicate include a variety of nudibranchs and snails.

Common Sea Pork *Aplidium stellatum*

Other Names Sea pork; formerly classified as *Amaroucium stellatum*.
Description This species' lobes are reddish-orange and arranged in star-like shapes. The colony is firm, rounded, and rubber-like in nature.
Size To 12" (30 cm) in diameter, 1" (25 mm) high.
Habitat On rocks and similar surfaces; low intertidal zone to depths of 25' (7.5 m).
Range Bay of Fundy to Gulf of Mexico.
Notes Members of the genus *Aplidium* often have an overall appearance that is similar to a slab of pork—hence their common name. Common sea pork builds a rather thick colony unlike another species found in the North Atlantic. Fragments of this species are sometimes found on beaches following a storm.

Similar Species **Northern sea pork *A. constellatum*** produces thin colonies that often have a coating of sand that adheres to the outer surfaces.

Carpet Tunicates *Didemnum* spp.

Other Name White crusts.

Description The white or brown to red or green colony is crust-like. Many tiny holes are present on the surface of the colony.

Size Normally to 4.75" (12 cm) in diameter, 0.25" (6 mm) high.

Habitat On rocks, wharves, and similar objects; low intertidal zone to depths of 1,350' (411 m).

Range Along the entire coast.

Notes Several species of carpet tunicates are present in the North Atlantic, and their colors vary widely. A microscope is necessary to identify the species. An orange to pink species, the invasive carpet tunicate was introduced to Maine in 1988; it can "carpet" large areas of the ocean floor. It was accidentally introduced from Asia or Europe and has spread rapidly ever since. Another species, green carpet tunicate *Didemnum listerianum* was also introduced into Atlantic waters. Introduced tunicates are now a global concern, as they often cover native organisms, disrupt the shellfish industry, and cause many other problems as well. Their proliferation is aided by a lack of natural predators in their new "homes."

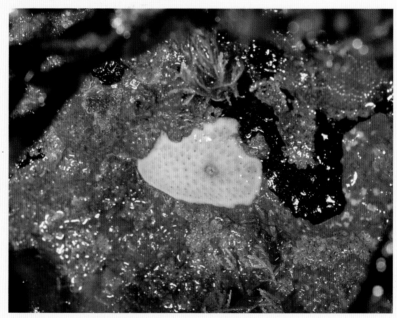

Egg case of Winter Skate *L*

FISHES

um Chordata

There are two major groups of fishes: cartilaginous fishes (Class Chondrichthyes) and bony fishes (Class Osteichthyes). Cartilaginous fishes have a skeleton made up of cartilage rather than bones and include the skates, rays, and sharks. As their name suggests, bony fishes have a bony skeleton. Nearly all fishes living today, approximately 21,000 species, are bony fishes. All fishes have gills to obtain oxygen from the water, a backbone surrounding the spinal cord, and single-loop blood circulation. Other creatures also found in the Phylum Cordata include mammals, birds, reptiles, and amphibians. Various fishes have been harvested by humans for millennia, and fish are one of humankind's more important foods, but few intertidal species have ever been harvested in temperate areas.

Cartilaginous Fishes
(Class Chondrichthyes)

Little Skate (Egg Case) *Leucoraja erinacea*

Other Names Common skate, summer skate, hedgehog skate; formerly classified as *Raja erinacea*.

Description The egg case is brownish, changing to black when dry. The capsule's exterior is very smooth and leathery, with long tendrils or "horns" at each corner. The length of the tendrils is greater than the length of the capsule.

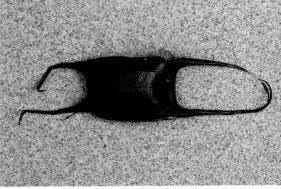

Size Fresh egg capsule 2.1–2.5" (53–64 mm) long, 1.4–1.9" (35–48 mm) wide (not including the tendrils). Dried purses are significantly smaller.

Habitat Often found washed up on exposed sandy beaches.

Range Gulf of St. Lawrence to Virginia.

Notes Eggs of little skate are laid year-round in pairs, buried in the sand. A total of 5 to 6 months is normally required for the eggs to hatch, but during colder months this time can be extended to 10 months. Empty egg cases are often found on the beach, where they are often referred to as "mermaid's purses." This is the most common species of egg case found washed up on the beaches of the Atlantic Northeast. Researchers have found that predation upon the little skate's egg cases is significant in some areas—up to 22% of the cases collected had holes drilled by various snails into the leathery covering of the egg case.

The adult little skate is flat and disk-like and reaches a length of 20" (51 cm); the dorsal surface is gray or brown. It feeds on crabs, shrimps, worms, tunicates, bivalves, and small fishes.

143

Winter Skate (Egg Case) *Leucoraja ocellata*

Other Names Big skate; spotted skate; eyed skate; formerly classified as *Raja ocellata*.

Description The egg case is greenish brown, changing to brown or black when dry. The capsule's exterior is smooth and leathery and has tendrils at each corner. The length of the tendrils is greater than the length of the capsule. A fibrous mat is attached to both edges of the "purse" (one or both may break off while on shore).

Size Fresh egg capsule 2.5–3.4" (64–86 mm) long, 1.4–1.9" (44–52 mm) wide (not including the tendrils). Dried egg cases are significantly smaller.

Habitat Often found washed up on exposed sandy beaches.

Range Gulf of St. Lawrence to North Carolina.

Notes The identification of skate egg cases or purses is best made with a combination of identifying features rather than by size alone. This is due to the fact that the purses shrink significantly as they dry—often more than 30%. Female skates anchor the tendrils or "horns" of each egg case to seaweed so that the capsule remains in place.

The adult winter skate is flat and disk-like and reaches a length of 36" (91 cm); the dorsal surface is light brown, and several eye spots are often present. This species also has more teeth than does little skate. The diet is very similar to that of little skate, but rock crabs and squid are their preferred prey.

Similar Species The egg cases of **barndoor skate *Raja laevis*** are yellowish or greenish brown, drying to black. The purse is large in size, from 4.7–5.1 inches (12–13 cm) long with 4 tendrils that are shorter than the capsule. This is the largest skate found in the Atlantic Northeast. Additional skates are also present in the North Atlantic, but they are not coastal species and as a result their egg cases are not likely to be found washed ashore.

Bony fishes (Class Osteichthyes)

Shorthorn Sculpin *Myoxocephalus scorpius*

Other Names Daddy sculpin, black sculpin, Greenland sculpin.
Description The dorsal surface ranges in color from reddish to green or brown with various mottling or bars. The ventral side is yellowish to whitish. Large blotches are found on the undersides of males. Its body tapers strongly, which makes this species look "front heavy." The anal fin is comprised of 13 or 14 rays.
Size To 20" (50 cm) long.
Habitat On rocky shores and estuaries; low intertidal zone to depths of 360' (110 m).
Range Arctic to New Jersey.

Notes Shorthorn sculpin is a remarkable creature: its blood contains two types of antifreeze proteins, which enable it to remain in tidepools and similar locations at temperatures near freezing. Other fishes, including the grubby (see under Similar Species), have also been identified to have similar proteins. The shorthorn sculpin dines on worms, crabs, sea urchins, and other invertebrates.
Similar Species **Grubby *Myoxocephalus aenaeus*** is similar in shape and coloration but only reaches 6" (15 cm) in length. It can be identified by counting a total of 10 or 11 anal fin rays.

Rock Gunnel *Pholis gunnellus*

Other Names Rock eel, tansy, butterfish.

Description The reddish to yellowish or greenish body is elongated and has small pectoral fins. Dark spots are found along the back and on the dorsal fin. A dark bar often runs from behind the mouth through the eye and eventually leads to the dorsal fin.

Size To 8″ (20 cm) long.

Habitat On rocky shores, in tidepools, and under seaweed; low intertidal zone to depths of 600′ (182 m).

Range Labrador to Delaware Bay.

Notes Rock gunnel is covered with a thick slime layer that is likely useful in escaping from predators but probably more useful in keeping this species moist while out of water. This species leaves tidepools for deeper waters in the North Atlantic from December through to March. In fact, all Atlantic Northeast intertidal fishes are only found in tidepools during the warmer months of the year, due to the cold winters. In other areas with warmer winters, it is common to observe intertidal fishes in tidepools year-round. Rock gunnel is known to reach 4 years of age.

Flat-tube Sea Lettuce *Ulva linza*

SEAWEEDS
Phyla Chlorophyta, Ochrophyta, and Rhodophyta

S eaweeds are algae (pronounced "AL-jee") or singular alga (pronounced "AL-guh") that are present in the oceans. Algae can be separated into two types based on size; micro-algae and macro-algae. Seaweeds are macro-algae that can be further divided into three different types: green algae, Phylum Chlorophyta; brown algae, Phylum Ochrophyta; and red algae, Phylum Rhodophyta. These divisions are based upon the presence of different pigments and the way in which they store their energy.

Reproduction is extremely complicated in the world of algae. Algae produce unicellular spores that can germinate and grow on their own. These are unlike plant seeds because plant seeds are complex, multicellular structures. Life cycles of algae often include a large obvious sporophyte (asexual) form and a smaller gametophyte (sexual) phase. This sequence is referred to as an alternation of generations. These generations can be similar in structures. In the life cycle of red algae there are three separate phases, whereas there are only two in others. As well, there is often no regular pattern of succession from one phase to the next. The mechanisms by which the gametes find each other also vary with each life cycle. In a few brown seaweeds, research has shown that female gametes can produce pheromones (scent attractants) that attract male gametes to increase the chances of fertilization.

Seaweeds have been used by man for thousands of years and are a valued commodity in world trade. Today they are harvested globally for a wide range of uses including food, shaving foams, fabric dyes, and much more. This multi-billion dollar industry has experienced phenomenal growth.

GREEN ALGAE
Phylum Chlorophyta

G reen seaweeds are normally bright green in color. Green algae can be unicellular, multicellular, and colonial. Most green algae are freshwater species, with a mere 13% being marine. Marine algae tend to remain in the upper levels of the oceans reaching to depths of approximately 3.3' (1 m). Near the sea surface, their ability to obtain sunlight for photosynthesis is greatly enhanced. Like green plants, they contain chlorophyll as the dominant pigment, which is responsible for their color. Chlorophyll converts sunlight energy into sugars and stores it, as in all green plants, in the form of starch.

Maiden Hair Sea Lettuce *Ulva intestinalis*

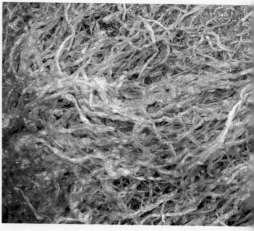

Other Names Hollow green weed, hollow green algae, green grass seaweed, maiden hair; formerly classified as *Enteromorpha intestinalis*.
Description The bright green elongated tubes are smooth overall, normally unbranched, and grow in clusters.
Size To 16" (40 cm) long, occasionally to 3.3' (1 m), 0.5" (12 mm) wide.
Habitat On rocks, sand, mud, wharves, and in tidepools; high intertidal zone to shallow subtidal.
Range Arctic to the South Carolina.
Notes Common periwinkle (p. 68) is often found grazing on maiden hair sea lettuce, which is one of its preferred foods. This cosmopolitan alga is composed of a tube that is a single cell thick and often bleached white by the sun. This species is often present where fresh water channels reach the ocean. When viewed underwater in a tidepool, bubbles may be observed inside the tubes. These help it stay afloat.

Common Sea Lettuce *Ulva lactuca*

Other Name Sea lettuce.
Description This bright green, sheet-like alga shows ruffled edges.
Size To 24" (60 cm) long, 6" (15 cm) wide.
Habitat On rocks, in tidepools, or an epiphyte (lives on other seaweed species); low intertidal zone.
Range Entire East Coast.
Notes Common sea lettuce is present in sites that have variable salinity. It is also often present in areas that are high in nitrogen, including polluted areas. The size of the blades produced is often massive in such areas. Sea lettuce (*Ulva* sp.) has the consistency of wax paper, which permits the tidepooler to view his or her fingerprints indistinctly through it (see similar species below). Around the globe, sea lettuce is eaten in soups, salads, and many other dishes.

Similar Species Green laver *Monostroma oxyspermum* is thinner (only 1 cell thick) and often compared to the thickness of tissue paper. A tidepooler can clearly see his or her fingerprints through it. Green laver grows to reach 8" (20 cm) in length. Other species of sea lettuce may also be encountered, but a microscope is required for their identification.

149

Flat-tube Sea Lettuce *Ulva linza*

Other Name Formerly classified as *Enteromorpha linza*.

Description The bright green blades are ribbon-like with wavy edges and often twisted spirally. This species is tubular with a tapering stipe, and the upper portion is flattened.

Size To 16" (40 cm) long, 1" (2.5 cm) wide.

Habitat On rocks; high intertidal zone.

Range Gulf of St. Lawrence to South Carolina.

Notes Flat-tube sea lettuce is a distinctive alga that is identified with its distinctive wide, hollow, tube-like filaments. Under ideal conditions during the summer months, this species may grow to form a band just below the rockweed zone. This species is absent in the fall, whereas maiden hair sea lettuce is found year-round.

Scientists have recently made major taxonomic changes to species in the sea lettuce clan, *Ulva* spp., Contemporary DNA studies, along with earlier molecular and culture research, confirms that the tubular species previously included in the genus *Enteromorpha* are best placed in the genus *Ulva*—just as Linnaeus, the father of scientific classification, had originally believed.

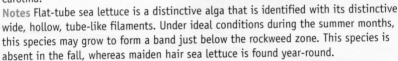

Green Beaded Filaments
Chaetomorpha melagonium

Other Name Green cord seaweed.

Description The appearance of this yellow-green species is filament-like, stiff, unbranched, and bead-like.

Size To 12" (30 cm) long.

Habitat On rocks and in tidepools; low intertidal zone to shallow subtidal.

Range Arctic to New Jersey.

Notes Due to the thin nature of this alga, this cold water species often goes unnoticed. Its thallus consists of a single row of large cells easily viewed with the naked eye. The large cells of green beaded filaments are often studied by scientists because they are easy to work with and view under a microscope.

Similar Species **Green tangled filaments *Chaetomorpha linum*** is another filament-shaped coarse alga that is unbranched. It resembles fishing line and grows to 4" (10 cm) long. It is commonly found in tangles. The yellowish-green cells can be viewed with a hand lens. Additional similar species may also be encountered. A microscope is required for correct identification.

Green Rope Seaweed *Acrosiphonia* spp.

Other Names *Codiolum* spp.; formerly classified in the genus *Spongomorpha*.
Description The green rope-like filaments have hooked branches that become twisted and tangled.
Size To 4" (10 cm) long.
Habitat On exposed rocks and in tidepools; mid- to low intertidal zones.
Range Arctic to New Jersey.
Notes The rope-like stands of green rope seaweed occur in only the gametophyte (sexual) stage of its life cycle. The sporophyte (asexual) stage looks very different, so much so that it was originally described as another species of *Codiolum* when first discovered. The sporophyte (asexual) stage is illustrated here. Several species of green rope seaweed may be encountered, but a microscope is required for their specific identification.

Sea Staghorn *Codium fragile*

Other Names Green fleece, dead man's fingers.
Description The green to yellow-green thallus is cylinder-shaped with a dense, felt-like surface. Each branch is divided with several regular or irregular divisions.
Size To 36" (91 cm) long, 0.75" (19 mm) wide.
Habitat On rocks, shells, and similar sites; mid-intertidal zone to shallow subtidal.
Range Maine to North Carolina.
Notes Originating from Europe, sea staghorn has slowly expanded its range from Long Island, where it was first discovered in 1957. This species is comprised of microscopic fibers running lengthwise that branch and rebranch to eventually turn outward and become swollen at the tips. Only the tips of the fibers bear its green color, signifying

where photosynthesis takes place. Because these fibers are so dense, sea staghorn absorbs a high volume of water and can become very heavy as a result. This species is often found washed up on the beach.

151

Tufted Sea Moss *Cladophora rupestris*

Other Name Mermaid's hair.

Description The dark green filaments are densely branched and appear moss-like. The filaments are smooth and stiff but not bead-like.

Size To 24" (60 cm) long.

Habitat On rocks; low intertidal zone to shallow subtidal depths.

Range Gulf of St. Lawrence to Massachusetts.

Notes The fronds of tufted sea moss are easily separated apart since they lack hooks. This characteristic is easily viewed with a hand lens. This common species is one of several sea mosses found on the Atlantic coast. The dense filament nature of sea moss enables it to hold large volumes of water, preventing it from drying out when the tide recedes.

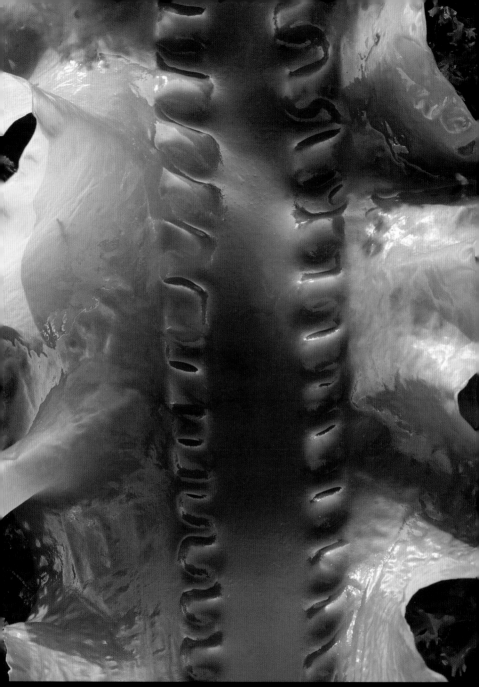

Sugar kelp *Saccharina latissima*

BROWN ALGAE
Phylum Ochrophyta

All brown algae are multicellular, and almost all species are marine. They were formerly considered to be part of the phylum Phaeophyta but are now placed in Class Phaeophyceae in the Phylum Ochrophyta.

Not all brown seaweeds are brown: they may be yellowish, blackish, or greenish as well. This is a result of the blending of the various pigments present. Fucoxanthin is the dominant pigment, although others are present, including chlorophyll. Fucoxanthin is a golden-brown pigment. Brown algae store energy in the form of a polysaccharide called laminarin. Large brown seaweeds are often referred to as kelp.

Brown seaweeds produce two compounds that are used in the manufacture of commercial goods—algin (an emulsifier) and fucans (slime of kelp—for possible future medicines).

Tufted Fringe *Elachista* spp.

Other Names Little seaweed; also known as *Elachistea* spp.
Description The brownish filaments form a dense cluster. Mature specimens harbor a second type of shorter filament that forms a dense cluster at the base of the tuft. These clusters are not visible but feel like a hard, hatpin-sized knob.
Size To 0.6" (16 mm) high.
Habitat On seaweeds; mid- to low intertidal zone.
Range Arctic to Massachusetts.
Notes This tiny seaweed is commonly found as an epiphyte attached to knotted wrack (p. 162), rockweed (p. 160), and other coarse algae. It grows vegetatively during the summer months and fruits during the autumn and winter. This beard-like seaweed is considered more advanced than other similar-looking species because it has developed two types of filaments with differentiated tissues.

Sea Cauliflower *Leathesia difformis*

Other Names Sea potato, cauliflower seaweed, brain seaweed, golden spongy cushion, rat's brain; also classified as *Tremulla difformis*.

Description This unusual yellowish-brown alga is best described as roughly spherical in shape, convoluted, hollow, and spongy.

Size To 5" (12 cm) in diameter.

Habitat Exposed and protected rocky areas in all intertidal zones. It is also epiphytic, growing on other species of algae.

Range Newfoundland to North Carolina.

Notes When this species was first described by the famous botanist and taxonomist Carolus Linnaeus, it was thought to be a jelly fungus because of its unusual shape. Sea cauliflower is solid when young but becomes hollow as it matures. It is found in many parts of the world, including the Pacific, Europe, and Chile.

Coarse Ribbon Weed *Punctaria plantaginea*

Description This alga is dark brown overall, with a leather-like blade that lacks a midrib. The blade tapers gradually to its short stipe, giving rise to a pad-like holdfast.

Size To 12" (30 cm) long.

Habitat On rocks, in tidepools, and occasionally epiphytic on other seaweeds; low intertidal zone to shallow subtidal depths.

Range Arctic to Chesapeake Bay.

Notes Appropriately named, ribbon weeds (*Punctaria* spp.) move in tidepools like ribbons waving in the wind. This is an annual species that disappears during the winter months. Coarse ribbon weed becomes somewhat ragged and darker or blackish as it ages.

Similar Species Delicate ribbon weed *P. latifolia* is lighter in color with a thinner, delicate blade that ends abruptly on a very short stipe and reaches a total length of 6" (15 cm). This alga is commonly found attached to eelgrass (p. 175) and large algae.

155

Stringy Acid Weed *Desmarestia viridis*

Other Names Soft sour weed, sea sorrel.

Description This alga is light to dark brown when in water and green when out of water. Comprised of many slender branches, it has a soft, bushy appearance with an opposite branching pattern from a central axis.

Size To 24" (60 cm) long.

Habitat On rocks or wood and in tidepools; low intertidal zone to shallow subtidal depths.

Range Arctic to New Jersey.

Notes Stringy acid weed produces sulfate ions inside its cells, and when plant cells are damaged the sulfate ions react with seawater

to produce sulfuric acid. This is a strong acid that dissolves tissues, including its own and those of any other algae nearby. It is also known to dissolve the calcium carbonate in the teeth of sea urchins. This is thought to deter grazing by green sea urchins (p. 136). This species has a sour smell when out of the water.

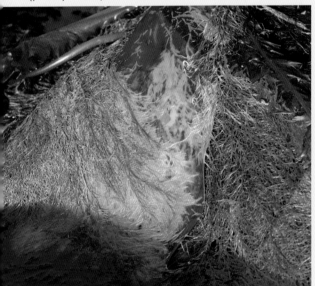

**Similar Species Wiry acid weed *Desmarestia aculeate* ** has a stiff appearance with an alternate branching pattern from a central axis. It is found from the Arctic to Long Island Sound. Some of the common names for this species show a great deal of imagination: witch's hair, crisp color changer, and landlady's wig.

The high acid content of stringy acid weed is evident on the kelp behind this acidic species.

Sausage Seaweed *Scytosiphon lomentaria*

Other Names Sausage weed, whip tube, leather tube, soda straws.
Description The golden brown to olive thallus (entire plant) is slender and hollow with constrictions at regular intervals.
Size To 24" (60 cm) long.
Habitat On rocks; mid- to low intertidal zone.
Range Subarctic to Florida.
Notes Well named, sausage seaweed resembles a chain of sausages and is not likely to be confused with other algae. Sausage seaweed may be found in two phases, the upright or sausage-shaped one and an encrusting form that clings tightly to rocks. The upright phase is formed during winter and is replaced with its prostrate counterpart in summer. This alga is found around the globe.

Rough Cord Weed *Chorda tomentosa*

Other Names Cord weed, rough hollow weed.
Description The thallus (whole plant) is brown, unbranched, and slender. Very fine dark brown to black hairs cover its surface.
Size To 3' (90 cm) long.
Habitat On rocks, docks, and pilings; low intertidal zone to shallow subtidal waters.
Range Labrador to Long Island.
Notes The tiny hairs that cover the surface of this whip-like species give it a gritty appearance. This annual is present during the winter and spring. It may be found washed up on shore after a storm or attached to a wharf piling at low tide. If only all seaweeds were this easy to identify!

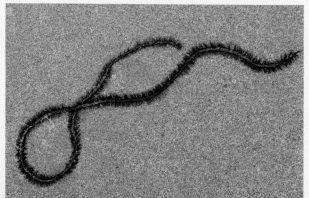

Similar Species **Smooth cord weed *Chorda filum*** is a similar species that grows to 16' (5 m) long with an overall smooth exterior and colorless hairs that are shed. It can be found from the Arctic to Long Island Sound at the low intertidal zone to subtidal depths.

157

BROWN ALGAE

Sugar Kelp *Saccharina latissima*

Other Names Southern kelp, common southern kelp; formerly classified as *Laminaria saccharina, L. agardhii*.

Description The dark brown to yellowish-brown blade changes its appearance as it develops. During winter, the blade is thick and strap-like without a midrib. In summer, two parallel "tire-tracks" are found in the mid-blade along with ruffled edges. Its holdfast is root-like.

Size To 10′ (3 m) long.

Habitat On rocks, pilings, and ledges; low intertidal zone to shallow subtidal depths.

Range Arctic to New Jersey.

Notes The name sugar kelp refers to the fact

that this species contains mannite, a sugar alcohol that gives it a sweet taste. It is used as a stabilizing agent for some of our sweeter treats—candies, puddings, and ice creams—and simply as a food in Japan. It is a good source of vitamin C, iodine,

protein, and calcium when added to casseroles or Asian dishes, for instance.

This impressive kelp is only found at the lowest of tides or washed ashore from subtidal depths. Recent DNA studies have determined that this species is much different, at the molecular level, from other members of the genus *Laminaria*. As a result, sugar kelp and a few other species have been reclassified in the genus *Saccharina*, a classsification that was used previously. This distinctive species is also present in Europe.

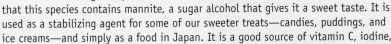

Finger Kelp *Laminaria digitata*

Other Name Horsetail kelp.

Description The blade of the dark brown to olive brown thallus is split into 6 to 30 finger-like sections. The stalk is stiff and wood-like.

Size To 6.5' (2 m) long.

Habitat On exposed rocks; low intertidal zone to shallow subtidal depths.

Range Arctic to Long Island Sound.

Notes Finger kelp prefers to live in areas with strong currents and cold water. The scientific name of finger kelp is an easy one to remember: digitata refers to the digits or fingers. Under the right conditions this kelp sometimes forms large patches. Finger kelp is also found in Russia and Europe, where it is harvested.

Winged Kelp *Alaria esculenta*

Other Names Edible kelp, dabblerlocks; formerly classified as *Laminaria esculenta*.

Description The brown elongated blade of this alga has a distinct midrib. A series of bladelets are also present near its root-like holdfast.

Size To 6.6' (2 m) long.

Habitat On the rocks of exposed shorelines and in tidepools; low intertidal zone to shallow subtidal depths.

Range Arctic to Long Island Sound.

Notes A series of reproductive bladelets, called sporophylls, extend from the lower portions of the winged kelp's stipe. These smaller blades resemble wings and are the origin of its common name. The scientific name esculenta means "tasty." This alga is one of several species of kelp that are edible. Winged kelp is perfect for soups and delicious raw in salads. Other palatable kelps include sugar kelp (p. 158) and finger kelp (above).

Sieve Kelp *Agarum cribrosum*

Other Names Sea colander, devil's aprons, shotgun kelp; formerly classified as *A. cribrosum*.

Description The dark brown to reddish blade is supported by a midrib. Each blade is perforated with many small round to oval holes spread over its entire surface.

Size To 6.5′ (2 m) long.

Habitat On rocks of protected shorelines and in tidepools; low intertidal zone to subtidal depths.

Range Arctic to Cape Cod, Massachusetts.

Notes The unique blades of this distinctive species are often found washed ashore from subtidal depths. Research on the Pacific coast has shown that this alga is avoided by urchins and often forms large stands as a result. In Alaska this species is known to live up to 6 years.

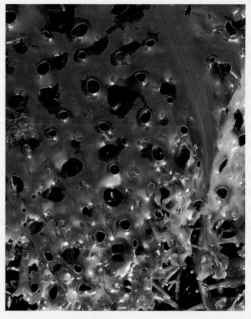

Northern Rockweed *Fucus vesiculosus*

Other Names Rockweed, bladder wrack.

Description The golden-yellow to dark green blades divide dichotomously (equally) and possess a midrib. Pairs of pea-shaped air bladders are found within the blade when present and a disk-shaped holdfast.

Size To 39″ (1 m) long.

Habitat On rocks, pilings, and wharves; mid- to low intertidal zone.

Range Arctic to North Carolina.

Notes Northern rockweed is the most common of several rockweeds found along the Atlantic coast. The paired air bladders, within the blade, help to identify this species. Receptacles or swollen reproductive structures that contain mucilage are often found on the tips of the blades of most *Fucus* during winter and spring. If a receptacle is opened, it is yellowish-orange in males and green in females. When ripe, each receptacle releases gametes into the water at high tide.

Spiral Rockweed *Fucus spiralis*

Other Name Spiraled wrack.
Description The yellowish to green blades divide dichotomously (equally), and a prominent central midrib is present. The receptacles normally have a flange-like ring of tissue on their outer edge. No bladders are present, and a disk-shaped holdfast keeps the alga in place.
Size To 3' (.9 m) long.
Habitat On rocks; high intertidal zone.
Range Arctic to North Carolina.
Notes Spiral rockweed is always found in the high intertidal zone with fronds that lack bladders. It is not always spiraled as its species name suggests. Beware too, that it often hybridizes with northern rockweed (p. 160). This alga is also found in the Pacific, Europe, and Africa.
Similar Species **Toothed Rockweed *F. serratus*** is similar except that its blades have a saw-toothed edge. It can be found in the mid-intertidal zone from the Gaspé Peninsula to Nova Scotia.

Flat Rockweed *Fucus distichus*

Other Names Popping wrack; formerly *F. evanescens*; the scientific name is occasionally misspelled *F. distichous*.
Description The green blades have flat receptacles that are not much thicker than the blades themselves. A midrib is present, but air bladders are not present.
Size To 24" (60 cm) long.
Habitat On rocks; low intertidal zone to shallow subtidal depths.
Range Arctic to New York.
Notes Flat rockweed is easy to identify by virtue of its distinctive receptacles. It may be found in both exposed and protected shorelines. This rockweed is found much lower in the intertidal shoreline than other species living in this zone. In fact, it is often found partially or totally submerged at low tide.

Knotted Wrack *Ascophyllum nodosum*

Other Name Rock-
weed.

Description The
green fronds of this
alga are round to
oval in shape with
elongated green
floats and yellow
receptacles. Its
branching is irregu-
lar, and stems form a
disk-shaped holdfast.

Size To 10′ (3 m)
long.

Habitat On rocks
in mud shorelines;
mid- to low intertidal
zone.

Range Arctic to New
Jersey.

Notes In many areas of our coastline knotted wrack is the dominant species of algae.
It does not easily establish itself on bare rock, but where other algal species are
present, it is able to establish itself. It is the final stage of succession of algae in the
intertidal zone of the Atlantic Northeast. Knotted wrack is long-lived—typically to
12 years, and there are records of this species surviving to an amazing 23 years. As

a result of this longevity,
it is the dominant species
of seaweed of many rocky
shores. Knotted wrack is
abundant and harvested
in the Atlantic Northeast
and in Norway, Ireland, and
Iceland. Its uses include
emulsifiers, thickening
agents, animal fodder, and
fertilizers.

This species is often the
host to a species of red
alga called wrack fringe
tubeweed (p. 172).

Wrack Fringe Tubeweed, *Vertebrata lanosa* growing on Knotted Wrack, *Ascophyllum nodosum*

Red seaweeds make up the greatest number of macroalgae on the globe. Members of this group reach the greatest depths of the ocean for seaweeds—one Caribbean species is known to survive at depths of up to 884′ (268 m).

Depending on the pigments present, red seaweeds may appear to be purple, red, pink, brown, green, or yellow. The overall red coloration is due to the pigment phycoerythrin (means "algal red") as well as phycocyanin (means "algal blue"). These pigments are able to absorb the light that penetrates deeper into the ocean water depths. Energy is stored in the form of a starch that man can digest and that is similar to that found in green plants.

Agar and carrageenan are emulsifiers that are often present in the cells of many red algae, and these are harvested commercially.

Purple Laver *Porphyra umbilicalis*

Other Names Laver, nori.
Description The purplish to purplish brown thallus is comprised of a single paper-thin sheet. A small disk-like holdfast keeps it attached to a rock.
Size To 14″ (35 cm) long.
Habitat On rocks, pebbles, and similar objects; high intertidal zone to shallow subtidal depths.
Range Arctic to Virginia.
Notes Purple laver is the most abundant laver found in the region. Lavers resemble colored wax paper—an easy way to describe their thalli. All laver is edible and is highly regarded for its edibility. It is commonly used as a complement to sushi. Research has shown that laver is high in iron and protein and low in sodium. The life cycle of laver involves two phases: a conspicuous blade form and a microscopic form sometimes referred to as the conchocelis phase. Once the large blades of laver are finished for the season, they disappear and the second microscopic phase takes over, with spores totally replacing them.

Rosy Laver *Porphyra miniata*

Other Names Laver, nori.
Description The rosy to rosy-purple thallus is comprised of a single rounded paper-thin sheet.
Size To 12" (30 cm) long.
Habitat On rocks, pebbles, and other seaweeds; mid-intertidal zone to depths of 33' (10 m).
Range Arctic to Virginia.
Notes The leafy thalli of rosy laver are not present year-round as they are with purple laver (p. 164). The ruffled blades are only observed from

March through to August. It grows on rocks as well as branching coraline alga (p. 167) and at the base of kelp fronds. Rosy laver is normally found at lower levels in the intertidal zone than purple laver.
Similar Species Dulse *Palmaria palmata* (p. 171) is fairly thick and has finger-like extensions of the thallus.

Twig Seaweed *Polyides rotundus*

Other Name Goat tang.
Description The dull red stalks turn black when they dry. The cylindrical stalks are slender, stiff, and branch 6–8 times. The disk-like holdfast keeps it in place.

Size To 12" (30 cm) high.
Habitat On rocks; low intertidal zone to depths of 66' (20 m).
Range Arctic to Long Island.
Notes Twig seaweed may only be observed at the lowest of tides. This common species prefers deeper water and is distinctive with its twig-like cartilaginous fronds originating from its single stipe. The species name *rotundus* refers to the round or spherical nature of its branches.

Red Crust Alga *Hildenbrandia rubra*

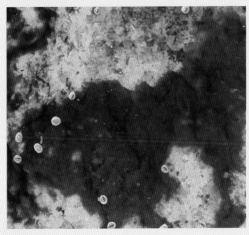

Other Names Shiny red crust. red rock crust; formerly classified as *H. prototypus* or *H. rosea*.

Description The bright red to brownish-red covering is thin, crust-like, non-calcareous, and tough in nature. Irregularly shaped patches are formed on rocks and shells.

Size Normally to 3" (76 mm) in diameter; however, in subtidal situations, several individuals may fuse to reach 39" (1 m) or more.

Habitat On rocks, shells, and in tidepools; high intertidal zone to depths of 90' (30 m).

Range Arctic to Florida.

Notes Red crust alga often goes unnoticed at the seashore, as it often appears to be part of the rock to which it is attached. It prefers tidepools and stable rocks that are not prone to movement. This perennial species is also found in the Caribbean, Europe, and West Africa. At present its sexual reproduction is unknown. Other similar species may also be encountered.

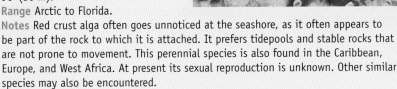

Coralline-crust Algae *Clathromorphum* spp.

Other Name Coralline alga.

Description The color varies from yellowish-pink to purplish-pink. This thin, crust-like species starts life with a smooth appearance and becomes very irregular and imbricate as it ages.

Size Normally to 4" (10 cm) in diameter; however, this species often overlaps with other individuals to produce larger sizes.

Habitat On rocks, shells, and tidepools; low intertidal zone to depths of 50' (15 m).

Range Labrador to Gulf of Maine.

Notes Coralline-crust algae is a calcareous species that produces some truly beautiful patterns on the rocks to which it adheres. A camera or paintbrush is ideal for recording this species' designs, as it cannot be removed from its substrate. This species also looses its fabulous color when removed from its habitat and left in the sun. The tortoiseshell limpet (p. 64) is a specialized feeder, with iron-capped teeth, that eats this algae.

Knobby Coralline-crust Alga
Lithothamnion graciale

Other Names Stone scrub, nobby red crust.

Description The pink to dull rose color often bleaches to white. This crustose alga is covered with rounded lobes on the surface.

Size To 12" (30 cm) in diameter; 0.75" (2 cm) thick.

Habitat On rocks, shells, and in tidepools; low intertidal zone to depths of 180' (55 m).

Range Arctic to Massachusetts.

Notes Knobby coralline-crust alga is a very easy calcareous alga to identify with its nipple-like protuberances. Its crust is formed from calcium and magnesium

carbonate. Its conceptacles (sunken cavities where the reproductive structures are located) are produced from spring to early winter. Coralline algae in general are among some of the longest-lived algae known—some examples as old as 50 years old have been recorded.

Branching Coralline Alga *Corallina officinalis*

Other Name Coral weed.

Description The pink to purplish-red fronds are tipped with white. This calcareous species is branching and comprised of many bead-like segments that often form tufts.

Size To 6" (15 cm) high.

Habitat On rocks or shells and in tidepools; low intertidal zone to depths of 50' (15 m).

Range Labrador to the Caribbean Sea.

Notes The beads of this species are calcified except at the joints. There the lack of calcification enables free articulating movement of its fronds in water. The graceful beauty of branching coralline alga is best viewed when it is found growing in a deep tidepool, where larger, intact individuals can often be studied. This seaweed was widely used as a vermifuge (for expelling parasitic intestinal worms from the human body) until the eighteenth century.

167

Bushy Red Seaweed *Cystoclonium purpureum*

Description The thalli are dark purple to reddish-brown with a firm but fleshy texture. Reddish cystocarps or reproductive bumps are often present. The main stipe is wider in diameter than the abundant fine branches, resulting in an overall bushy appearance.
Size To 24" (60 cm) long.
Habitat On rocks, shells, and in tidepools; low intertidal zone to depths of 45' (13.5 m).
Range Newfoundland to New Jersey.
Notes The bushy red seaweed is a species that prefers sheltered waters. Its genus *Cystoclonium* is translated "branches with bladders," which refers to the reproductive structures found on its many branches. A unique variety of this species var. *corrhosum* may also be encountered. This variety features many branches that have become spirally coiled.

Variable Tube Seaweed *Devaleraea ramentacea*

Other Name Formerly classified as *Halosaccion ramentaceum*.
Description The red to purple blades fade to rust or golden brown with time. The blades are hollow with a smooth surface, often with at least a few lateral branchlets that resemble hairs.
Size To 16" (40 cm) long.
Habitat On rocks of very exposed coastal shorelines and tidepools; low intertidal zone to depths of 33' (10 m).

Range Arctic to Massachusetts.
Notes Just as the common name suggests, this highly variable species may resemble several other seaweeds including sausage seaweed (p. 157) and smooth cord weed (p. 157). It may display several branchlets or none, and its width ranges from narrow or cord-like to broad as is illustrated here. Sexual reproduction is unique in this genus due to the passive, non-flagellated sperm cells. This species is also found in Alaska.

Irish Moss *Chondrus crispus*

Other Names Pearl moss, carrageen moss, carrageen, jelly moss.
Description The reddish-brown to purple or yellowish-green blades often appear iridescent blue when viewed underwater. Each flattened blade is dichotomously (equally divided) branched, one or more times. This species often produces tufts, and a disk-like holdfast keeps it in place.
Size To 13" (32 cm) long.
Habitat On rocks, shells, and in tidepools; low

intertidal zone to depths of 230' (70 m) and occasionally in mid-intertidal tidepools.

Range Newfoundland to New Jersey.
Notes This well-known red alga is a perennial that requires 3–5 years to reach maturity. Male plants are separate from female plants. This species is quite variable in appearance due to wave action, grazing pressure, and other factors. In exposed sites this alga tends to branch closer to the substrate with a shorter height. At sheltered sites, the talli tend to be taller and have wider blades.

Irish moss is extensively harvested for carrageen—an important thickening agent for foods such as ice cream, syrups, puddings, and dairy products. Irish moss is very nutritious and used in the preparation of blancmange—a white dessert jelly served with chocolate or fresh fruit. This species is also found in Europe.
Similar Species **False Irish moss *Mastocarpus stellatus*** (p. 170) is normally covered with papillae or small bumps.

The smooth surface of the thallus helps to identify this species as Irish moss.

False Irish Moss *Mastocarpus stellatus*

Other Names Blade Phase: Tufted red weed; formerly classified as *Gigartina stellata* or *G. cornopifolia*; scientific name previously spelled *Mastocarpus stellata*.
Crust Phase: Formerly classified as *Petrocelis cruenta*.
Description Blade Phase: The purplish brown blades are flattened and dichotomously branched one or more times. The surfaces of the blades

Blade phase.

are usually covered with papillae or small bumps on female plants. Male plants lack papillae and are generally rare. Dense tufts are often formed, arising from a disk-like holdfast.
Crust Phase: The purplish-black crust is tar-like and smooth on the surface, with a more or less random shape.
Size Blade Phase: To 8" (20 cm) high.
Crust Phase: To 4.75 (12 cm) in diameter.
Habitat On rocky shores; low intertidal zone to shallow subtidal depths.
Range Newfoundland to Rhode Island.
Notes As its common name suggests, this species is very similar to and often confused with Irish moss (p. 169). They are often collected together when harvested for carrageenan. The life cycle of false Irish moss consists of two distinct stages or phases. These phases are easily distinguished visually: a blade phase and a crust phase. The blade phase is often found immediately above Irish moss in the low intertidal zone because it is more frost tolerant. The tar-like crust phase is often referred to as the Petrocelis-phase because it was formerly believed to be a separate species named *Petrocelis cruenta*.

Tar or crust phase.

Dulse *Palmaria palmata*

Other Name Formerly classified as *Rhodymenia palmata*.

Description Thallus is comprised of several separate leaflets attached to its short stipe. The leather-like blades are wide and divided into finger-like extensions.

Size To 20" (50 cm) long.

Habitat On rocks, pebbles, and other seaweeds; low intertidal zone to depths of 10' (3 m).

Range Arctic to New Jersey.

Notes Dulse is well-known for its wide-ranging uses as a food. It is often used in soups, chowders, sandwiches, and salads, or added to pizza dough. Dulse can be sun-dried and eaten as it is, or it may be ground to make flakes or a powder. It may also be pan fried quickly with butter into rather tasty chips or baked in the oven covered with cheese and salsa. It is very rich in trace elements and vitamins, particularly vitamin A. Dulse contains large amount of several carbohydrates which can form up to 30% of the dry weight and may account largely for its palatability.

The life cycle of dulse is somewhat different in the world of algae. Asexual plants and the male gamete-producing stage have been very well known for a long time, but the female gamete-producing stage was never found. Eventually female gamete-producing individuals were discovered to be minute in relation to the large male gamete-producing stage, and the full life cycle was found to be unique to dulse and other members of the genus Palmaria. This species is a common intertidal seaweed in the northern part of its range. Farther south, it grows in deeper subtidal waters.

Wrack Fringe Tubeweed *Vertebrata lanosa*

Other Names Tubed red weed, tubed weed; formerly classified as *Polysiphonia lanosa*; occasionally misspelled *P. lanora*.

Description The black to reddish-brown thallus is cylindrical, densely tufted, and repeatedly branched. It is attached to its host by creeping rhizoids with branches that penetrate into the host plant.

Size To 3" (7.5 cm) high.

Habitat On seaweeds on wave-exposed shorelines; high to low intertidal zone.

Range Arctic to Long Island.

Notes Wrack fringe tubeweed is a tough, hemiparasite (semiparasite) of seaweeds, especially knotted wrack (p. 162). Occasionally northern rockweed (p. 160) also acts as a host. Wrack fringe tubeweed is a hemiparasite because it lacks a fully developed haptera system (root-like system) and as a result must form connections with other seaweeds. This species is partially dependent on the host species to obtain amino acids, phosphates, and other minerals. In addition, there is also a mutual exchange of fixed carbon compounds through photosynthesis. This alga is often found growing on the damaged fronds of its host.

Smooth Cordgrass *Spartina alterniflora*

FLOWERING PLANTS

Phylum Anthophyta

Flowering plants are vascular plants, the most advanced and most diverse of all the plant groups, with well developed systems for conducting food and water. As their name suggests, they possess a flower or flowers, although seashore species normally lack bright colors. The flower, when pollinated, matures into fruit. Additional parts of a typical flowering plant include the leaves, stem and roots. At the seashore, this amazing group of plants has developed modifications to survive the salt spray, drifting sands, poor soils, flooding, and other challenges. There are approximately 250,000 species of flowering plants described in the world.

Smooth Cordgrass *Spartina alterniflora*

Other Names Salt-marsh cordgrass, cordgrass, tall cordgrass, salt marsh grass, erect cordgrass.
Description The dark green leaves are long and tapering with maroon colored sheaths at their bases. The flower clusters reach up to 12" (30 cm) long.
Size To 78" (2 m) high; leaves greater than .2" (.5 cm) wide.
Habitat In mudflats; mid-intertidal zone.
Range Newfoundland to Florida.

Notes Smooth cordgrass has the greatest salt tolerance among grasses and commonly grows at the lowest levels in the intertidal zone. Its large leaves are the most conspicuous part of this species. Its inconspicuous green flowers bloom in late in the summer. This species stabilizes mudflats and aerates the heavy soils. During the winter months, only stubble remains, with the upper parts being washed away. Early colonists used this species to thatch the roofs of their cottages.
Similar Species **Salt meadow cordgrass *S. patens*** grows above smooth cordgrass in the high intertidal zone. It is a shorter species that reaches a height of 24" (60 cm) with narrower leaves that are rolled. This species, also called salt meadow hay, is less salt tolerant.

Pickleweed *Salicornia* spp.

Other Names Glasswort, saltwort, sea
asparagus, samphire.
Description A green, fleshy succulent
with jointed stems and leaves reduced
to minute scales.
Size To 12" (30 cm) tall; stems may trail
to 39 " (1 m).
Habitat On sheltered shores at the high
tide mark; especially common in saltwater marshes and tideflats.
Range New Brunswick to Florida.
Notes Pickleweeds have been used
traditionally as a food worldwide for
many years. They are often pickled
(hence their name) as well as used as a
fresh (and very salty) veggie. Pickleweed
also has been used externally in the
treatment of arthritic pain, rheuma-
tism, aches, pains and swellings. Much
confusion surrounds the identification of
pickleweed species that may be encountered in North America.

Common Eelgrass *Zostera marina*

Other Names Eel-grass, eel grass.
Description The long blade-like leaves are green and characteristically flat from a
rhizome with its roots growing in sand or mud.
Size To 8' (2.5 m) long.
Habitat In quiet bays with a sand or mud bottom; low intertidal zone to water 100'
(30 m) deep.
Range Arctic to South Carolina.
Notes Common eelgrass grows where it can be totally submerged in seawater. This
plant grows in large beds where a wide variety of marine creatures take residence.
Its roots stabilize the substrate, ensuring that the area is protected from erosion. In

the early 1930s, com-
mon eelgrass experienced
catastrophic losses due to
a blight. The Atlantic eelgrass limpet *Lottia alveus*
once made this plant its
host from Labrador to New
York. Today the Atlantic
eelgrass limpet is extinct,
likely due to the drastic
reduction of its host species, common eelgrass.

175

Seaside Plantain *Plantigo maritima*

Other Names Sea plantain, seashore plantain, goose-tongue.

Description Flowers are greenish and inconspicuous in dense spikes and the leaves are green changing to golden brown in the fall. This is a perennial herb with fleshy tissues that grow from a taproot.

Size To 10" (25 cm) high.

Habitat Among and between rocks; salt spray zone.

Range Arctic to Virginia.

Notes The young salty leaves of this species were eaten by various native peoples of North America. Seaside plantain can flourish in amazingly small amounts of soil collected in crevices of large seashore boulders. This species is widespread in Eurasia, Patagonia, the Galapagos Islands, and along the Pacific coast of North America.

Maritime Sunburst Lichen *Xanthoria parietina*

The phylum Ascomycotina (sac fungi) includes both lichens and cup fungi but not true fungi. Lichens are a unique working partnership between two organisms: an algae component that photosynthesizes, much as higher plants do, and a fungus, which provides protection. There are two types of fruiting bodies present on seashore lichens: apothecia (disk-like structures) and perithecia (sacs under the surface).

Lichens are nature's pioneers, breaking down rock and making the way for the colonization of other plants. Encrusting lichens grow very slowly—as little as 1mm a year to perhaps as much as 1cm per year. If this estimate is accurate, it is likely that some individual lichens that are with us today were also growing while woolly mammoths roamed Earth 9,000 years ago!

Maritime Sunburst Lichen *Xanthoria parietina*

Other Names Wall lichen, shore lichen.

Description The thallus (the vegetative body) is orange to yellowish-orange or greenish-orange with broad lobes. Apothecia (disk-like structures) are broad with dark orange disks, and the rim is the same color as its thallus.

Size Rosettes to 4" (10 cm) in diameter, apothecia to .3" (8 mm) in diameter.

Habitat On rocks; salt spray zone.

Range Gulf of St. Lawrence to New Jersey.

Notes Maritime sunburst lichen is a common species that is present along the seashores of the Atlantic northeast. The apothecia (disk-like structures) are nearly always present on this vibrant species. A hand lens greatly aids in observing the details here and for all lichens. Due to its color it was formerly believed to be a cure for jaundice. In the Pacific Northwest this lichen is found on the bark of hardwoods.

Black Seaside Lichen *Verrucaria maura*

Other Names Sea tar, black lichen, wart lichen.
Description The thallus ranges in color from black to dark brown with numerous cracks and ridges. Small rounded black pimples are present created by perithecia (embedded sacs that contain spores).
Size To a near-continuous strip along the shoreline up to 39" (1 m) wide.
Habitat On rocks; high intertidal zone to salt spray zone.
Range Arctic to Massachusetts.
Notes This lichen is widespread along much of the coastline. It is easily missed because it looks much like the rock to which it is

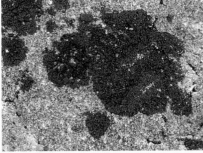

so closely attached. The *Verrucaria* clan is one of few lichen genera that contain perithecia (fruiting bodies in sacs under the surface). This widespread species is found in Europe as well as the Pacific coast of North America.
Similar Species Smooth seaside lichen *V. mucosa* is found on both coasts of North America. It has a smooth, thick, olive-green thallus that appears gelatinous when wet. It is not as common as black seaside lichen.

Close-up of black seaside lichen.

Sulphur Dust Lichen *Chrysothrix chlorina*

Other Name Formerly classified as *Lepraria chlorina*.
Description The thallus is sulphur colored and comprised almost entirely of soredia or powdery granules. Apothecia are absent.
Size To several square yards (meters) in size.
Habitat On shaded rocks; above the salt spray zone.
Range Nova Scotia to Massachusetts.
Notes Sulphur dust lichen does not produce apothecia or disk-like structures in North America. Instead it reproduces entirely by the spreading of soredia or powdery gran-

ules. This species contains the pigments calycin and vulpinic acid that give it its color. This lichen is found at the seashore as well as in boreal situations. It can also be found in rare situations on the bark of conifers. The sulphur dust lichen is also found along the Pacific coast of North America and Europe.

Hooded Rosette Lichen *Physcia adscendens*

Description The thallus is grayish on the dorsal side with a black underside, and it tends to lie flat against its substrate. Hood-shaped swellings at the tips bear very small soredia or powdery granules.
Size Rosettes to 2" (5 cm) in diameter.
Habitat On rocks; salt spray zone.
Range Newfoundland to New Jersey.

Notes Hooded rosette lichen is present across much of the North American continent, growing primarily on trees. Although it does not favor the seashore, it is tolerant of the salt in this area. This common species is found in agricultural and urban areas primarily on the bark and twigs of trees at low elevations.

Blue-gray Rosette Lichen *Physcia caesia*

Other Names Powder-black lichen, blue-grey rosette lichen, gray rock lace, blue-gray blister lichen.
Description The dorsal side of the thallus is bluish-gray to yellowish-white. The underside varies from white to brown with various colored rhizines (root-like extensions). Apothecia (disk-like fruiting bodies) are rare. The distinctive soredia (powdery granules) are black or brown with a frost-like appearance.
Size Rosettes to 3" (8 cm) in diameter.

Habitat On rocks; salt spray zone.
Range Arctic to Connecticut; circumpolar in the northern hemisphere.
Notes Blue-gray rosette lichen is a foliose species that favors rocky sites beneath bird perches. It is found in a number of additional habitats and not restricted to the beach. This species is so adaptable that it is even found in alpine regions.

Rachel Carson Salt Pond Preserve, Maine.

Selected Sites for
Intertidal Exploration

Atlantic Northeast

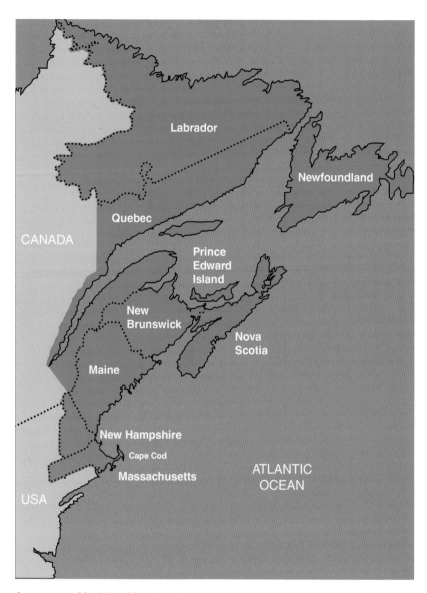

Range covered in this guide —Canada to Cape Cod.

The intertidal sites listed below are just a few of the many public sites suitable for seashore exploration. Always respect the creatures you are viewing by replacing the rocks the same way they were found and by returning the creatures to their homes. Also respect the environment you are visiting. The seashore is a rugged yet fragile environment. In virtually all of these areas, flowers, trees, insects, birds, and mammals can also be studied.

Canada

NOVA SCOTIA

Cranberry Cove, Nova Scotia.

Fox Harbour Provincial Park, NS

Site Description: Mud beach.
Nearest Town: Wallace, NS
Notes: The area surrounding this park is picturesque. Fox Harbour Provincial Park is a day-use park that features a mud bay where eelgrass (p. 175) grows and several marine creatures make their homes, including northern quahog (p. 105), softshell-clam (p. 106), Atlantic jackknife-clam (p. 102), longwrist hermit (p. 121), and iridescent sandworm (p. 50). Occasionally clam diggers try their hand at gathering northern quahogs here. If you plan to dig for clams, be sure that you have checked for closures, limits, and license requirements.
For More Information:
Nova Scotia Provincial Parks
http://parks.gov.ns.ca/ourparks.asp

Tide Pond, Brier Island, NS

Site Description: Rocks, sand, mud, and tidepools.
Nearest Town: Digby, NS
Notes: The setting of this site makes the trip to Brier Island most worthwhile. This is a wonderful intertidal site for a multitude of seaweeds. Tide Pond is a local area just off Western Light Road, accessed from Wellington Street. The invertebrates found here include northern sea star (p. 131), European green crab (p. 125), green sea urchin (p. 136), and Atlantic rock crab (p. 123). Other activities that are offered on the island include whalewatching and birdwatching boat tours, which provide excellent opportunities to view birds and whales in season. Check locally for details.
For More Information:
Brier Island, Nova Scotia
http://www.brierisland.org/

Beautiful Cove, Long Island, NS

Site Description: Rocks and tidepools.
Nearest Town: Digby, NS
Notes: Fabulous tidepools at this site are filled with coraline algae and other algae, depending upon the intertidal level. A few of the marine creatures found here include the green sea urchin (p. 136), Atlantic rock crab (p. 123), painted anemone (p. 32), and European green crab (p. 125). As with all tidepools, many creatures are not noticeable until they feel safe. This means that the longer you wait quietly at the edge of the tidepool, the better chance you have to view more marine creatures. Patience is often rewarded.

Cottage Cove Provincial Park, NS

Site Description: Rocks, mud, and tidepools.
Nearest Town: Middletown, NS
Notes: Cottage Cove Provincial Park is a popular picnic site. The varied marine life found here includes Atlantic dogwinkles (p. 75), in a variety of colors, and Acadian hermits (p. 121) in the tidepools. Other species here include common jingle (p. 95), barnacle-eating dorid (p. 83), silver-spotted anemone (p. 33), European green crab (p. 125), and rock gunnel (p. 146). As is true for the entire Gulf of Fundy, this site experiences huge tidal fluctuations. It is an amazing place to observe the speedy return of the tidal waters. Camping can be found nearby.
For More Information:
Nova Scotia Provincial Parks
http://parks.gov.ns.ca/ourparks.asp

Hunts Point, NS

Site Description: Rocks, sand, and tidepools.
Nearest Town: Liverpool, NS
Notes: Hunts Point has an excellent white sandy beach for sunbathing and a rocky edge. Located in the heart of the village of Hunts Point, it makes a quiet get-away spot for a relaxed day at the beach. Among the marine species that reside here are silver-spotted anemone (p. 33), painted anemone (p. 32), short plumose anemone (p. 34), shag rug nudibranch (p. 88), northern sea star (p. 130), green sea urchin (p. 136), scud (p. 117), and rock gunnel (p. 146).

Cranberry Cove, NS

Site Description: Rocks and tidepools.
Nearest City: Halifax, NS
Notes: Cranberry Cove lies near Peggy's Cove—one of the more popular tourist attractions of the Halifax area. Be sure to take a trip to the lighthouse while in the area. The slippery rocks near the lighthouse are posted against entry, but Cranberry Cove is a nearby sheltered area that can be safely explored. This site is near the Memorial to Swiss Air Flight 111. Some of the marine organisms that may be found here include short plumose anemone (p. 34), painted anemone (p. 32), northern sea star (p. 130), and sinistral spiral tubeworm (p. 55). Seaweed here is abundant, slippery, and must be "navigated" with caution.
For More Information:
Peggy's Cove Preservation Area
http://www.oceanstone.ns.ca/preservationarea/

Kingsport Flats, NS

Site Description: Mud and sand beach.
Nearest Town: Wolfville, NS
Notes: Kingsport Flats, as this area is often called locally, is a great mud beach in the Minas Basin that is often visited by commercial worm diggers. Here the tide exposes a wide stretch of intertidal flats. A few creatures found here include eastern mud snail (p. 81), three-lined basketsnail (p. 78), and common periwinkle (p. 68). For those interested in finding marine worms, there are many that can be found here, such as the collared bambooworm (p. 52), two-gilled bloodworm (p. 49), and the milky ribbon worm (p. 45). Fish, including the rock gunnel (p. 146), often become stranded in pools when the tide goes out. Be sure to bring along rubber boots for navigating the mud at this site!

PRINCE EDWARD ISLAND

Cabot Beach Provincial Park, Prince Edward Island.

Cabot Beach Provincial Park, PE

Site Description: Sandy beach.
Nearest Town: Kensington, PE
Notes: The protected waters of Malpeque Bay are found at Cabot Beach Provincial Park. Here you may take a stroll along the beautiful beach and find northern moonsnail (p. 73) or sevenspine bay shrimp (p. 118) at the water's edge. If you look for shells, you may find those of northern quahog (p. 105), softshell-clam (p. 106), and Atlantic jackknife-clam (p. 102), while a longer walk may produce Forbes' sea star (p. 129) or eastern mud snail (p. 81) on the far side of the peninsula. Camping is also offered at this popular park during the summer months.
For More Information:
Prince Edward Island Provincial Parks
http://www.gov.pe.ca/visitorsguide/index.php3?number=1010978

Prince Edward Island National Park, PE

Site Description: Sandy beaches.
Nearest City: Charlottetown
Notes: Prince Edward Island is well known for its wild, windswept beaches. This park has extensive sandy beaches, great locations to look for various shells

washed ashore. Greenwich, Stanhope, and Cavendish beaches have many of the same shells: Atlantic surfclam (p. 99), common Atlantic slippersnail (p. 70), blue mussel (p. 92), Northern moonsnail (p. 73), as well as cast exoskeletons of American lobster (p. 119). After a storm, additional species are also often tossed ashore here. A visitor center is located at Greenwich.

For More Information:
Prince Edward Island National Park
http://www.pc.gc.ca/pn-np/pe/pei-ipe/index_E.asp

NEW BRUNSWICK

Green Point and Letite Lighthouse, New Brunswick.

Green Point, NB

Site Description: Rocks, sand, mud, and tidepools.
Nearest Town: St. George, NB
Notes: If you visit Green Point in the fog, you will hear the fog horn from Letite Lighthouse here. Green's Point is also known by as Letite Point and Mascabin Point. This area includes both sheltered and exposed areas. Creatures that call his area home include Forbes' sea star (p. 129), Atlantic blood star (p. 131), painted anemone (p. 32), barnacle-eating dorid (p. 83), red-finger aeolis (p. 87), tortoiseshell limpet (p. 64), and Gould's trumpetworm (p. 53). At very low tides, green sea urchins (p. 136) or northern sea stars (p. 131) may be observed feeding on blue mussel (p. 92). Local universities use this area for their intertidal studies.

For More Information:
Green's Point Light, L'etete Passage, New Brunswick
http://www.cyberlights.com/lh/canada/greenpoint.htm

SELECTED SITES

Maces Bay, NB

Site Description: Sand, mud, and some rock.
Nearest Town: St. George, NB
Notes: Maces Bay is an extensive site often visited by locals who dig for softshell-clams (p. 106). If you plan to collect clams, be sure to check for local regulations, limits, and closures. Marine life found at this site includes Atlantic dogwinkle (p. 75), rough periwinkle (p. 67), northern moonsnail (p. 73), and blue mussel (p. 92). For those who wish to view seaweeds, this is a great site to check after a storm. Here various algae cover the bedrock, and eelgrass (p. 175) beds are also present.

New River Beach Provincial Park, NB

Site Description: Rocks, sand, and tidepools.
Nearest Town: St. George, NB
Notes: New River Beach Provincial Park is a marvelous place to enjoy a beautiful sandy beach as well as to camp and hike. The sandy beach is an excellent site to walk along the beach and look for shells washed ashore from recent storms. Shells that may be found here include ten-ridged whelk (p. 78), waved whelk (p. 77), and three-lined basketsnail (p. 78). For those who wish to discover the world of the rocky shore, a nature hike to Barnaby Head will lead you to several sand and cobble beaches by way of a boardwalk area. Be mindful that rough trail sections can be slippery when wet. Rocky intertidal areas can be found at the edges of the coves along the route. Some of the creatures you may encounter include painted anemone (p. 32), Atlantic dogwinkle (p. 75), northern sea star (p. 130), and green sea urchin (p. 136). Areas of slippery seaweeds must be traversed to reach the low areas; take a slow approach to ensure good footing.
For More Information:
Provincial Parks - New Brunswick Tourism
http://www.tourismnewbrunswick.ca/en-CA/HNNationalAndProvincialParks/
HNPProvincial.htm

Irving Nature Park, St. John, NB

Site Description: Rocks, sand, and mud.
Nearest City: St. John, NB
Notes: Nestled in the city of St. John lies Irving Nature Park. This large park is popular with locals. It includes a rocky shoreline, mud shore, and saltmarsh estuary. The rocky section is mixed with sand and is the best location here for finding a variety of shells, including ten-ridged whelk (p. 78), common Atlantic slippersnail (p. 70), eastern oyster (p. 96), three-lined basketsnail (p. 78), and northern sea star (p. 130). During the summer, interpreters conduct guided walks

featuring the creatures found on the shore. Check locally for more information about event locations and times.
For More Information:
Irving Nature Park - New Brunswick Tourism
http://www.tourismnewbrunswick.ca/en-CA/Product/MunicipalPark.htm?pid=2077

Fundy National Park, NB

Site Description: Rocks, sand, and mud.
Nearest Village: Alma, NB
Notes: Fundy National Park is a great park to bicycle, hike, or camp. Freshwater wetlands, Acadian forest, bog, and intertidal shores are in close proximity here. A rocky intertidal site is located at Herring Cove, a quick drive from the visitor center. A variety of creatures make this location their home, including barnacle-eating dorid (p. 83), collared bambooworm (p. 52), Atlantic dogwinkle (p. 75), and northern rock barnacle (p. 112). Some of the shells on the shore are common jingle (p. 95) and striate cup-and-saucer (p. 70). If you wish to explore a mud shoreline, Alma Beach is the place. A parking lot is located beside the east park gate, from which it is an easy walk to the shore. Be careful not to get stranded on a temporary island while walking the mud beach. Here you may find the empty shells of northern moonsnail (p. 73), Stimpson whelk (p. 77), waved whelk (p. 77), common Atlantic slippersnail (p. 70), and three-lined basketsnail (p. 78).
For More Information:
Fundy National Park, NB
www.pc.gc.ca/fundy

Indian Point, NB

Site Description: Rocks, sand, mud, and tidepools.
Nearest Town: St. Andrews, NB
Notes: A mixture of mud and red rock are present at this unmarked site. Ask one of the friendly locals to confirm its location. A campground is situated next to the site for those who wish to "rough it" overnight in the area. At this site you are likely to find the softshell-clam (p. 106), Baltic macoma (p. 103), green sea urchin (p. 136), northern moonsnail (p. 73), and barnacle-eating dorid (p. 83). For those interested in shells, the smooth periwinkle (p. 66) is present here in an amazing array of colors: their empty shells may litter small sections of the shoreline by the hundreds.

SELECTED SITES

NEWFOUNDLAND, AND LABRADOR

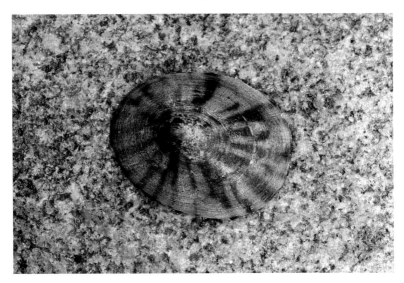

Tortoiseshell Limpet.

Terra Nova National Park, NF

Site Description: Rocks.

Nearest Town: Gander, NF

Notes: The shores of Newman Sound offer visitors a wonderful opportunity to view a variety of seashore creatures including tortoiseshell limpet (p. 64), rough periwinkle (p. 67), and green sea urchin (p. 136). Be sure to visit the visitor center that features various marine exhibits, aquariums, a touch tank, and a fixed underwater camera with a live link to the shore.

For More Information:

Parks Canada, Terra Nova National Park

http://www.pc.gc.ca/pn-np/nl/terranova/index_E.asp

United States

MAINE

Cobscook Bay State Park, Maine.

Mount Desert Island, Acadia National Park, ME

Site Description: Rocks and tidepools.
Nearest Town: Bar Harbor, ME
Notes: The Mount Desert Island section of Acadia National Park is a marvelous place to visit. Here a visitor may bike, hike, camp, picnic, or fish. For those wishing to visit tidepools, there are some excellent sites to explore. Check in with the visitor center for the latest update on the best locations for tidepool exploration. Creatures that may be found at this park include bread crumb sponge (p. 29), Atlantic dogwinkle (p. 75), Atlantic rock crab (p. 123), Jonah crab (p. 124), Atlantic hairy hermit (p. 122), northern red chiton (p. 62), and many more. Be sure also to ask at the visitor center about ranger-led shoreline activities while you are in the park.
For More Information:
Acadia National Park
http://www.acadia.net/anp/

Schoonic Peninsula, Acadia National Park, ME

Site Description: Rocks and tidepools.
Nearest Town: Winter Harbor, ME
Notes: Many people visit the Schoonic Peninsula to view the wild splendor of the coast. Schoonic Point is an excellent site to view storms, but intertidal studies are sometimes affected by these storms. Do not look for seashore creatures at the point itself; the sheltered areas on either side of the point are safer areas to view intertidal life. Some of the creatures you may observe include northern sea star (p. 130), green sea urchin (p. 136), barnacle-eating dorid (p. 83), European green crab (p. 125), Atlantic rock crab (p. 123), and bread crumb sponge (p. 29). The power of the waves here is often reflected in the bottoms of the tidepools, which may be covered in shell fragments.
For More Information:
Acadia National Park
http://www.nps.gov/acad/

Cobscook Bay State Park, ME

Site Description: Mud with rocky edges.
Nearest Town: Lubec, ME
Notes: Cobscook Bay State Park is a large, scenic area that offers a wide variety of recreational opportunities. Here you may camp, fish, or dig for clams. The campsites are large and the scenery spectacular. If you plan to harvest clams on the mud beaches, be sure to check on limits, closures, and sizes. This interdidal site is the home to waved whelk (p. 77), green sea urchin (p. 136), Baltic macoma (p. 103), blue mussel (p. 92), northern horsemussel (p. 94), and the everpopular softshell-clam (p. 106).
For More Information:
Maine Department of Conservation, Bureau of Parks and Lands
http://www.maine.gov/cgi-bin/doc/parks/find_one_name.pl?park_id=15

Quoddy Head State Park, ME

Site Description: Rocks and tidepools.
Nearest Town: Lubec, ME
Notes: This intertidal site is a slippery one, with the abundance of seaweeds covering every rock. Care must be taken to reach the lower sections of the beach. Tidepools hold a wide variety of treasures just waiting to be discovered: bread crumb sponge (p. 29), northern sea star (p. 130), and tortoiseshell limpet (p. 64) among them. A lighthouse next to this park is another of the area's attractions.
For More Information:
Maine Department of Conservation, Bureau of Parks and Lands
http://www.state.me.us/cgi-bin/doc/parks/find_one_name.pl?park_id=10

Moose Point State Park, ME

Site Description: Rocks, sand, and mud.

Nearest Town: Searsport, ME

Notes: Moose Point State Park offers a large grassed area for a variety of recreational activities as well as picnicking. At rock, sand, and mud shorelines, blue mussel (p. 92), common periwinkle (p. 68), northern sea star (p. 130), green sea urchin (p. 136), and European green crab (p. 125) are often observed. For those with a sharp eye, the test of a sand dollar (p. 137) or perhaps the empty shell of a softshell-clam (p. 106), Arctic hiatella (p. 107), or truncated softshell-clam (p. 107) may be found washed ashore.

For More Information:

Maine Department of Conservation, Bureau of Parks and Lands
http://www.state.me.us/cgi-bin/doc/parks/find_one_name.pl?park_id=19

Owls Head Light State Park, ME

Site Description: Rocks, sand, and tidepools.

Nearest City: Rockland, ME

Notes: Owls Head Light State Park is a popular day-use area for those wishing to visit the lighthouse. Intertidal areas are also present at this rocky site. Low tides reveal many small tidepools that harbor northern sea star (p. 130), daisy brittle star (p. 133), green sea urchin (p. 136), European green crab (p. 125), and Atlantic rock crab (p. 123). A few intertidal fishes are often observed here as well, including rock gunnel (p. 146). There are very steep areas in the park that are posted against entry. The view from the lighthouse is a fine way to appreciate the area.

For More Information:

Owl's Head Light
http://lighthouse.cc/owls/

Rachel Carson Salt Pond Preserve, ME

Site Description: Rocks, sand, and tidepools.

Nearest Town: Damariscotta, ME

Notes: The Nature Conservancy has set aside this preserve for scientific and educational purposes. This is the site where Rachel Carson conducted scientific studies for many years and eventually wrote The Edge of the Sea. Once the tide recedes, it reveals the salt pond, a quarter-acre tidal pond. This site hosts a wide array of intertidal creatures. By carefully lifting a rock, you may encounter a northern sea star (p. 130), Atlantic blood star (p. 131), daisy brittle star (p. 133), green sea urchin (p. 136), European green crab (p. 125), or Atlantic rock crab (p. 123). A variety of nudibranchs may also be observed, including bushy-backed nudibranch (p. 85). Because this is a preserve, all animals, plants, and rocks are protected by law.

SELECTED SITES

For More Information:
Rachel Carson Salt Pond Panorama
http://www.cnr.berkeley.edu/departments/espm/env-hist/espm160/assignments/carson/carson.htm
Trails.com
http://www.trails.com/tcatalog_trail.asp?trailid=CGN038-014

Reid State Park, ME

Site Description: Rocks, sand, and tidepools.
Nearest Town: Woolwich, ME
Notes: This site offers bicycling, picnicking, sunbathing, and cross-country ski-ing. At the seashore, excellent tidepools await those wishing to view into the marine world: painted anemone (p. 32), silver spotted anemone (p. 33), northern sea star (p. 130), hairy spiny doris (p. 83), and bushy-backed nudibranch (p. 85) may all be found here. Outside the tidepools, additional marine species that may be encountered include Atlantic dogwinkle (p. 75), tortoiseshell limpet (p. 64), and bread crumb sponge (p. 29). Many species of seaweed also make this intertidal site their home.
For More Information:
Maine Department of Conservation, Bureau of Parks and Lands
http://www.maine.gov/cgi-bin/doc/parks/find_one_name.pl?park_id=13

Two Lights State Park, ME

Site Description: Rocks and tidepools.
Nearest Town: Cape Elizabeth, ME
Notes: Two Lights State Park has a wild, exposed shoreline. Here you will find an extensive rocky area with tidepools and ledges made from metamorphic rock. The tidepools hold species such as blue mussel (p. 92), scud (p. 117), northern sea star (p. 130), and common periwinkle (p. 68). Various seaweeds are plentiful as well. The park has posted signs stating that the safe distance from the water is a minimum of 20 feet. It is important to heed these signs, as rogue waves may occur at any time, not just during storms.
For More Information:
Maine Department of Conservation, Bureau of Parks and Lands
http://www.maine.gov/cgi-bin/doc/parks/find_one_name.pl?park_id=28

Kennebunk Beach, ME

Site Description: Rocks and sand shore.
Nearest Town: Kennebunk Port, ME
Notes: The extensive Kennebunk Beach offers a protected shoreline site and one that is more exposed. The sand is mixed with mud, and the rocky areas include

rocks and boulders of all sizes. Empty shells found on the beach may include soft-shell-clam (p. 106), blue mussel (p. 92), Atlantic razor-clam (p. 100), northern horsemussel (p. 94), northern moonsnail (p. 73), and Atlantic dogwinkle (p. 75).
For More Information:
Discover Kennebunkport & Kennebunk Beach
http://www.kennebunkbeach.com/kennebunkport.htm

York Harbor, ME

Site Description: Rocks and sand shore.
Nearest City: York Harbor, ME
Notes: When surfers use the beach next to an intertidal area, you know the site can have strong waves. The presence of empty shells of the Atlantic surfclam (p. 99) caught among the rocks also indicates that this site is an exposed one. Other invertebrates that may be found on the rocks include northern sea star (p. 130), tortoiseshell limpet (p. 64), and Atlantic dogwinkle (p. 75).
For More Information:
York Main Beaches
http://www.yorkharborinn.com/area/beaches.htm

NEW HAMPSHIRE

North Hampton State Beach, New Hampshire.

Odiorne Point State Park, NH

Site Description: Rocks and tidepools.
Nearest Town: Rye, NH
Notes: This park protects an extensive intertidal site that provides a home to a wide variety of marine invertebrates. Here, northern sea star (p. 130) and Atlantic blood star (p. 131) are tidepool neighbors to barnacle-eating dorid (p. 83) and red-finger aeolis (p. 87). Many other species also make this park their home. This park is also the site for the Seacoast Science Center, where a number of marine displays are featured. Here many schoolchildren participate in outdoor education activities that feature the intertidal world.
For More Information:
Odiorne Point State Park, NH
http://www.nhstateparks.com/odiorne.html

North Hampton State Beach, NH

Site Description: Sandy beach and rock area.
Nearest Town: North Hampton, NH
Notes: Although this site is limited in size, it is one of many rocky areas that jut northward into the ocean. This site provides habitat for bread crumb sponge (p. 29), green sea urchin (p. 136), Atlantic dogwinkle (p. 75), and scud (p. 117).
For More Information:
North Hampton State Beach, NH
http://www.nhstateparks.com/northhampton.html

MASSACHUSETTS

Harding Beach, Cape Cod, Massachusetts.

Halibut Point State Park, MA

Site Description: Rocks and tidepools.
Nearest City: Gloucester, MA
Notes: Halibut Point State Park is an exposed site that features many tidepools in which various marine invertebrate species live. Blue mussel (p. 92) is abundant here, as are northern rock barnacle (p. 112), common periwinkle (p. 68), rough periwinkle (p. 67), and smooth periwinkle (p. 66). Waves can be dangerous here at times, so caution is advised. The best time to visit this site is at the lowest of tides.

An old abandoned quarry site, where 440-million-year-old granite was once quarried, is located here, and a small visitor center is open during the summer months.
For More Information:
Halibut Point State Park, MA
http://www.mass.gov/dcr/parks/northeast/halb.htm

Plum Cove, MA

Site Description: Sand with rocky edges.
Nearest City: Gloucester, MA
Notes: Plum Cove is a small, sheltered cove nestled in urban Gloucester. The marine life found here includes common periwinkle (p. 68), smooth periwinkle (p. 66), the tortioseshell limpet (p. 64), barnacle-eating dorid (p. 83), and rock gunnel (p. 146). Shells found on the beach indicate the area also supports northern moonsnail (p. 73) and blue mussel (p. 92).
For More Information:
Shore Diving – Plumb Cove
http://www.shorediving.com/Earth/USA_East/Massachusetts/Plum_Cove/index.htm

Brewster Sand Flats, MA

Site Description: Sand and mud seashore.
Nearest Town: Brewster
Notes: This site offers an opportunity to explore sand and mud flats in a sheltered environment. You must pass the stabilized dunes that are on the trail to reach the flats. Intertidal species here include northern quahog (p. 105) and softshell-clam (p. 106), whose empty shells are usually present in abundance. This is also an excellent place to find the empty egg cases of little skate (p. 143), sometimes by the hundreds.
For More Information:
Brewster Beaches
http://www.brewstercapecod.org/information/whattodo/beaches

Manomet Point, MA

Site Description: Rocky shore.
Nearest Town: Manomet, MA
Notes: Manomet Point is an excellent site to discover a wide range of marine life. In the pools you may find Asian shore crab (p. 126), northern sea star (p. 130), or common periwinkle (p. 68). Turn over a rock and you may discover an orange sheath tunicate (p. 140) colony attached tightly to the colorful rocks found here. The patterns they create are always a treat to view. This site is home to a world-class wildlife research facility, Manomet Center for Conservation Sciences.
For More Information:
Recreational Shellfish Area Map for Plymouth, Massachusetts
http://www.plymouth-ma.gov/Public_Documents/PlymouthMA_Harbor
http://www.manomet.org

Scituate Lighthouse, MA

Site Description: Rocky shore.
Nearest Town: Scituate, MA
Notes: The rocky coastline near Scituate, the site of numerous shipwrecks, provides homes for a variety of marine invertebrates, among them common periwinkle (p. 68), smooth periwinkle (p. 66), tortoiseshell limpet (p. 64), and Asian shore crab (p. 126). A few empty shells may also be found washed ashore here, especially those of blue mussel (p. 92).
For More Information:
Scituate Lighthouse, MA
http://www.lighthousefriends.com/light.asp?ID=469

Harding Beach, Cape Cod, MA

Site Description: Sandy beach.
Nearest Town: Chatham, MA
Notes: This wonderful sandy beach along Nantucket Sound is an excellent spot to take a walk at any time of year. During the winter months, many shells of various species are often tossed ashore after a storm. You may discover several exoskeletons or shells of Atlantic horseshoe crabs (p. 120) lying on the beach. Live individuals are also found at this location. Empty mollusk shells often found at this site include knobbed whelk (p. 79), bay scallop (p. 94), northern moonsnail (p. 73), and common Atlantic slippersnail (p. 70). The egg cases of knobbed whelk, channeled whelk (p. 80), and northern moonsnail are also often found here washed up on the beach.
For More Information:
Massachusetts Lighthouses
http://www.unc.edu/~rowlett/lighthouse/ma.htm

Cape Cod National Seashore, MA

Site Description: Sand and mud beaches.

Nearest Town: North Eastham, MA

Notes: The excellent sandy beaches of Cape Cod National Seashore are well known by many. These exposed waters, however, do not deposit many shells on the beach. On the other hand, the more protected waters of this spectacular landscape have other noteworthy marine life forms. Atlantic marsh fiddler (p. 127) and Atlantic sand fiddler (p. 127) crabs are found together in a sheltered mud bay (known as "The Gut") on the hiking trail to Great Island, which is no longer an island. This site has the northernmost population of these fiddler crabs, whose claw-waving antics can be amusing to watch. Be sure to stop in at the visitor center for more information.

For More Information:

Cape Cod National Seashore, MA
http://www.nps.gov/caco/

Selected References

Abbott, R. T. 1974. *American Seashells: The Marine Mollucsa of the Atlantic and Pacific Coasts of North America*. Van Nostrand Reinhold Co., New York, New York.

Bertness, M. D. 1999. *The Ecology of Atlantic Shorelines*. Sinauer Associates, Inc., Sunderland, Massachusetts.

Bigelow, H. B. and W. C. Schroeder. 1953. *Fishes of the Gulf of Maine*. United States Department of the Interior, Fishery Bulletin of the Fish and Wildlife Service 53, Washington, D.C.

Bird, C. J., and J. L. Mclachlan. 1992. *Seaweed Flora of the Maritimes 1. Rhodophyta – the Red Algae*. National Research Council of Canada, Halifax, Nova Scotia.

Bleakney, J. S. 1996. *Sea Slugs of Atlantic Canada and the Gulf of Maine*. Nimbus Publishing and The Nova Scotia Museum, Halifax, Nova Scotia.

Bousfield, E. L. 1960. *Canadian Atlantic Sea Shells*. National Museum of Canada, Ottawa, Ontario.

Brodo, I. M., S. D. Sharnoff, and S. Sharnoff. 2001. *Lichens of North America*. Yale University Press, New Haven, Connecticut.

Clark, A. M., and M.E. Downey. 1992. *Starfishes of the Atlantic*. Chapman and Hall, New York, New York.

Gibson, M. 2003. *Seashores of the Maritimes*. Nimbus Publishing Limited, Halifax, Nova Scotia.

Gosner, K. L. 1978. *Atlantic Seashore: A Field Guide to Sponges, Jellyfish, Sea Urchins, and More*. Houghton Mifflin Company, New York, New York.

Keates, H. 1995. *Beachcomber's Guide from Cape Cod to Cape Hatteras: Marine Life of Massachusetts, Rhode Island, Connecticut, New York, New Jersey, Delaware, Maryland, Virginia, and North Carolina*. Gulf Publishing Company, Houston, Texas.

Kingsbury, J. M., and P. Sze. 1997. *Seaweeds of Cape Cod and the Islands*. Bullbrier Press, Jersey Shore, Pennsylvania.

Lee, T. F. 1986. *The Seaweed Handbook: An Illustrated Guide to Seaweeds from North Carolina to the Arctic*. Dover Publications, New York, New York.

Martinez, A. J. 2003. *Marine Life of the North Atlantic: Canada to New England*. Aqua Quest Publications Inc., New York, New York.

Meinkoth, N. A. 1981. *The Audubon Society Field Guide to North American Seashore Creatures*. Knopf, New York, New York.

Pollock, L. W. 1998. *A Practical Guide to the Marine Animals of Northeastern North America*. Rutgers University Press, New Brunswick, New Jersey.

Rehder, H. 1981. *The Audubon Society Field Guide to North American Seashells*. Knopf, New York, New York.

Scott, W. B., and M. G. Scott. 1988. *Atlantic Fishes of Canada*. University of Toronto Press, Toronto, Ontario.

Sears, J. R. 2002. *NEAS Keys to Benthic Marine Algae*. Northeast Algal Society. Express Printing, Fall River, Massachusetts.

Smith, R. I. 1964. *Keys to Marine Invertebrates of the Woods Hole Region*. Contribution No. 11, Marine Biological Laboratory, Woods Hole, Massachusetts.

South, G. R. 1975. *Common Seaweeds of Newfoundland*. Oxen Pond Botanic Park, Marine Sciences Research Laboratory, Memorial University, St. John's, Newfoundland.

Taylor, W. R. 1957. *Marine Algae of the Northeastern Coast of North America*. University of Michigan Press, Ann Arbor, Michigan.

Watling, L., J. Fegley, and J. Moring. 2003. *Life Between the Tides: Marine Plants and Animals of the Northeast*. Tilbury House, Publishers, Gardiner, Maine.

Glossary

Acontia: Thin threads that containi nematocysts and that are emitted defensively by many anemones.

Alga (plural algae): Plants that live in an aquatic environment and lack a root system.

Antenna (plural antennae): A slender, sensory appendage that projects from the cephalic (head) area.

Aperture: The opening into which the entire body of a snail can withdraw.

Apex: The top of a shell in a snail, limpet, or other gastropod.

Apothecia: Disc-like vegetative fruiting bodies that produce spores in lichens.

Asci: Sac-like reproductive structures that hold ascospores.

Ascospores: Sexual spores in lichens that are found inside asci.

Atrial siphon: The outgoing or excurrent siphon of tunicates.

Atrium: A chamber of the heart.

Auricles: The wing-like projections on scallop shells.

Beak: The projecting part of the hinge in bivalves

Byssal threads: see Byssus.

Byssus: Tough silk-like threads secreted by a gland in the foot of some bivalves to anchor their valves to a solid substrate.

Callus: A tongue-like covering of the umbilicus.

Carapace: The hard covering or exoskeleton that covers the upper portion of a shrimp or crab.

Ceras (plural cerrata): The elongated projections found on the back of aeolid nudibranchs used in gas exchange as well as extensions of the digestive gland.

Cillia: Minute hair-like structures used for locomotion, food gathering, and other functions.

Cirrus (plural cirri): The modified legs of barnacles; soft hair-like or finger-like projections.

Ctenes: The comb plates of comb jellies.

Columella: The central axis of true snails.

Commensal: The relationship between two different organisms in which one benefits and the other is not affected.

Conceptacles: Sunken cavities where the reproductive structures are located in red algae.

Chondrophore: A spoon-shaped projection found near the hinge on one of the shells of a bivalve.

Cystocarps: The bump-like reproductive structures on seaweeds.

Detritus: Debris that contains organic particles.

Dextral: A right-handed spiral or clockwise coil.

Epiphyte: A plant that lives on another plant but not as a parasite.

Exoskeleton: An external skeleton, such as the shell of a crab.

External ligament: The portion of the ligament that is visible when a bivalve is closed.

Filter feeder: An organism that strains particles of food from the water.

Flagellum (plural flagella): The whip-like extensions found on some cells, used for motility and feeding.

Gametophyte: The sexual (gamete-forming) stage of algae.

Girdle: The muscular tissue that surrounds the eight valves of a chiton.

Gonads: Reproductive organs.

Haptera: The root-like portion of algae in one type of holdfast.

Holdfast: The root-like part of algae.

Issicles: Plate-like or spine-like structures found in echinoderms.

Ligament: The tough, elastic part of the hinge that joins the two valves of a bivalve.

Madreporite: The sieve plate or a porous plate that allows water to pass both in and out.

Mantle: A fold in the body wall that lines the shell of a mollusc. Also, the sac-like hood that is present behind the eyes of an octopus.

Midden: A pile of refuse.

Nematocyst: A cell that releases a stinging or entangling thread for the protection of jellies, sea anemones, and related organisms (Phylum Cnidaria).

Ocelli: Eyespots on ribbon worms.

Operculum: The calcareous or horn-like door that covers a snail for protection when it has retreated inside its shell.

Oral disk: A disk with a central mouth for feeding as found in sea anemones.

Osculum (plural oscula): The large pore through which water exits from a sponge.

Ostium: An incurrent pore through which water enters a sponge.

Pallial line: The line on the inner surface of the valves of bivalves that is present between the two large muscle scars.

Pallial sinus: The indentation at the hind end of the pallial line on the inner surface of the valves of bivalves.

Papillae: The finger-like projections used in respiration on the dorsal side of nudibranchs.

Parapodia: The lateral extensions on the side of each segment of segmented worms.

Pedicellariae: Pincer-like appendages found on sea stars and sea urchins.

Pelagic: Free-swimming in the ocean.

Pelvic fins: The pair of fins on fish that are found on the rear of the belly.

Periostracum: The thin skin-like coat of organic material secreted by various molluscs on the outside of their shells.

Perithecia: The embedded fruiting bodies in sacs under the surface of some lichens. Their openings often look like tiny dots on the surface.

Pholad: A bivalve that bores into clay or rock.

Planula: Free-swimming larvae of many cnidarians.

Polychaete: Segmented worms that have paddle-like appendages, well-developed sense organs, and many setae (hairs).

Polyp: An elongated individual organism (in the Phylum Cnidaria) with a mouth surrounded by tentacles at one end and attached to a substrate at the other end.

Proboscis: The organ found at the "snout" of ribbon worms that can be extended. Also, the anterior end of the digestive tract that can be found in some annelids; this organ can be everted. Also, a muscular tube found at the anterior end of the digestive tract in some snails used for feeding.

Radula: A toothed, tongue-like ribbon in the mouth of gastropods used to rasp food from a hard surface.

Rhinophore: A large pair of antennae-like sensory organs found on the head of nudibranchs.

Rhizines: The root-like extensions on the lower surface of lichens.

Roe: The eggs or ovaries of an invertebrate. Also, the eggs of fish.

Rostrum: An elongated, usually pointed structure found at the front of the carapace.

Sinistral: A left-handed spiral or counter-clockwise coil.

Soredia: Tiny granules on the surface of lichens that are used in asexual reproduction.

Spicule: A lime or glass rod that provides support for sponges.

Sporophyte: The asexual or vegetative stage of algae.

Stipe: The stalk of an alga.

Test: The round internal skeleton of the sea urchin or sand dollar.

Thallus (plural thalli): The main body of algae, lichens, and other organisms that lack roots. The holdfast or its equivalent is not included.

Umbilicus: The navel-like opening in the center of the columella, at the base of true snails.

Umbo or umbone: The "beak" or prominent portion of the hinge on a bivalve.

Valve: Shell. One of 2 calcareous coverings of a bivalve. Also, one of the 8 shells of a chiton.

Veliger: A larval mollusc with wing-like appendages.

Velum: A veil-like ring that hangs on the underside of a jelly.

Zooid: An individual bryozoan or moss animal within a colony.

Illustrations for Identification

The following illustrations represent most major groups of marine life found at the seashore. These labeled drawings are included here to aid in identifying the main features of each life form.

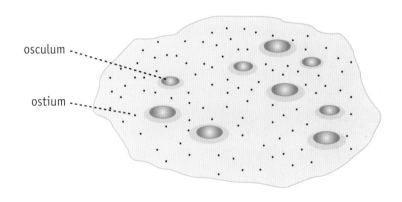

osculum

ostium

Sponge

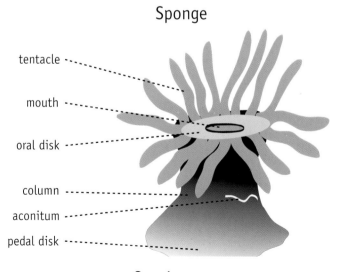

tentacle

mouth

oral disk

column

aconitum

pedal disk

Sea Anemone

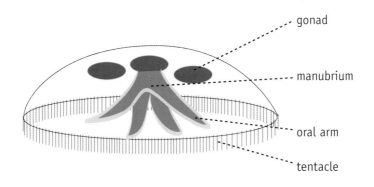

gonad

manubrium

oral arm

tentacle

Jelly

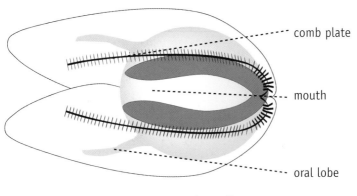

comb plate

mouth

oral lobe

Comb Jelly

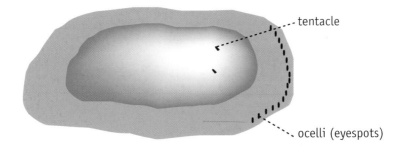

tentacle

ocelli (eyespots)

Flatworm

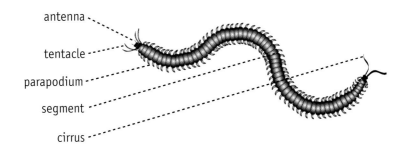

antenna
tentacle
parapodium
segment
cirrus

Segmented Worm

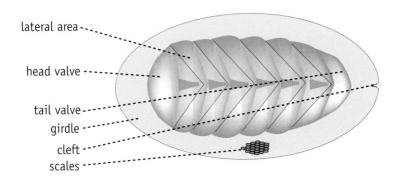

lateral area
head valve
tail valve
girdle
cleft
scales

Chiton (Dorsal View)

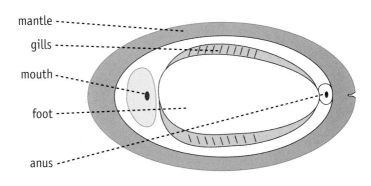

mantle
gills
mouth
foot
anus

Chiton (Ventral View)

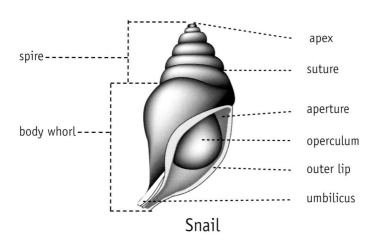

spire

apex

suture

aperture

operculum

outer lip

umbilicus

body whorl

Snail

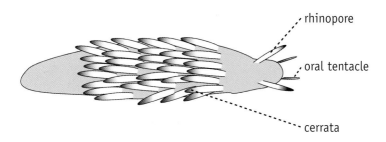

rhinopore

oral tentacle

cerrata

Aeolid Nudibranch

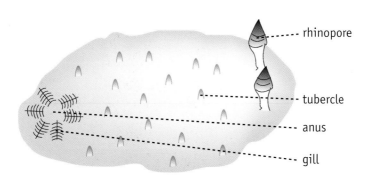

rhinopore

tubercle

anus

gill

Dorid Nudibranch

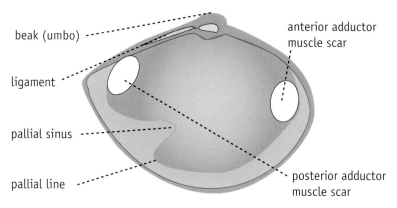

beak (umbo)

anterior adductor muscle scar

ligament

pallial sinus

pallial line

posterior adductor muscle scar

Bivalve (Shell interior)

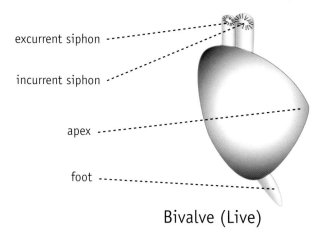

excurrent siphon

incurrent siphon

apex

foot

Bivalve (Live)

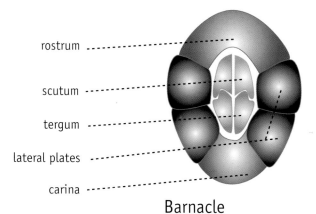

rostrum

scutum

tergum

lateral plates

carina

Barnacle

ILLUSTRATIONS

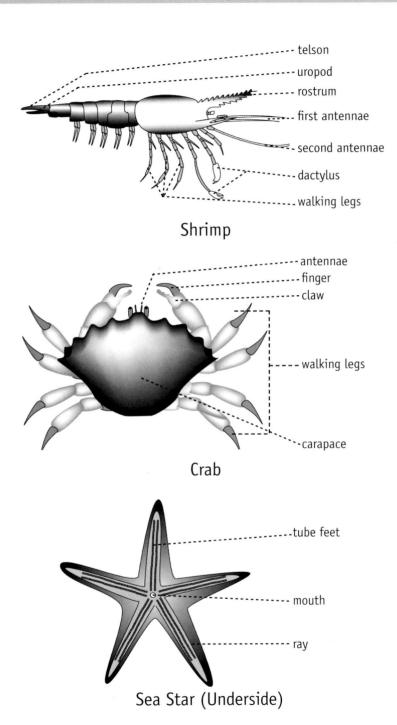

Shrimp

- telson
- uropod
- rostrum
- first antennae
- second antennae
- dactylus
- walking legs

Crab

- antennae
- finger
- claw
- walking legs
- carapace

Sea Star (Underside)

- tube feet
- mouth
- ray

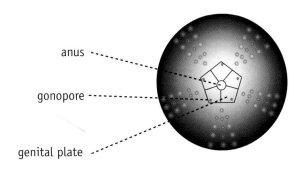

anus
gonopore
genital plate

Sea Urchin Test (Top view)

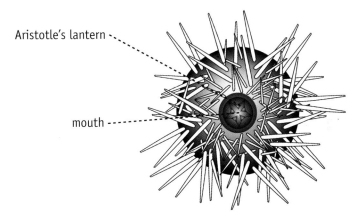

Aristotle's lantern
mouth

Sea Urchin (Bottom view with spines)

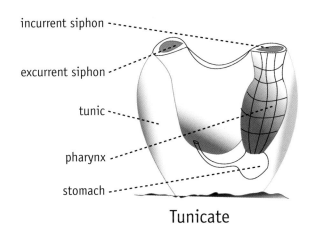

incurrent siphon
excurrent siphon
tunic
pharynx
stomach

Tunicate

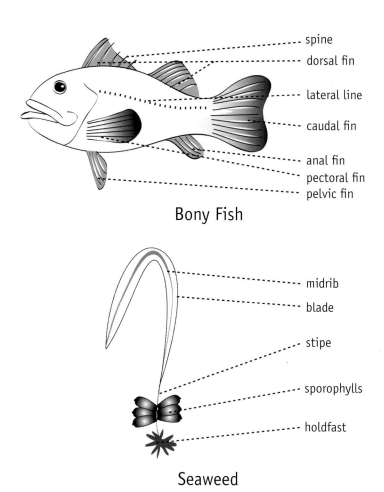

spine
dorsal fin
lateral line
caudal fin
anal fin
pectoral fin
pelvic fin

Bony Fish

midrib
blade
stipe
sporophylls
holdfast

Seaweed

Acknowledgments

I would like to thank several people who assisted with this project in so many ways. Without their help this project would not have been possible.

First and foremost, I would like to thank Robert Kirk at Princeton University Press for taking on this project. I would also like to thank Edward Brinkley for his careful and insightful editing.

A number of individuals were kind enough to freely give of their time and expertise to identify specimens or photographs, confirm identifications, review text, update current scientific names or otherwise assist with this project in additional ways. These include: Terri Bremer (Cape Cod Museum of Natural History, Brewster, MA), Evan Gwilliam (Cape Cod National Seashore, Wellfleet, MA), Andrew Hebda (Nova Scotia Museum of Natural History, Halifax, NS), Gretchen Lambert (California State University, Fullerton, CA), Charlene Mayes (University of New Brunswick, Fredericton, NB), Jon Norenburg (National Museum of Natural History, Washington, DC), Leslie Pezzack (Nova Scotia Museum of Natural History, Halifax, NS), Gerhard Pohle (Huntsman Marine Science Centre, St. Andrews, N.B.), Gary W. Saunders (University of New Brunswick, Fredericton, NB), Jim Simon (Fisheries & Oceans Canada, Halifax, NS).

Site suggestions and other helpful on-site assistance were freely given by many individuals within various organizations. These include: The naturalists (Nova Scotia Museum of Natural History, Halifax, NS), park staff (Reid State Park, ME), visitor center staff and volunteers (Cape Cod National Seashore, Wellfleet, MA).

The following individuals were also very kind to provide site suggestions; Anne Bardou (Fundy National Park, NB), Karen Townsend (Fundy National Park, NB).

Skilled photographers provided additional photographs. Their names appear below.

Photography Credits
All photographs are by J. Duane Sept except the following:

Joel Wooster 90T&B [file yoldia], 109T [great piddock]
USGS (United States Geological Survey) 126B [Asian shore crab]

To view additional images by J. Duane Sept visit:
http://www.septphoto.com

Index

dorid,
    barnacle-eating, 83
    white, 84
doris,
    hairy spiny, 83
    hairy, 83
    muricate, 84
    rough-mantled, 83
    yellow false, 84
dove-shell, lunar, 76
drill,
    thick-lip, 76
    thick-lipped, 76
dulse, 171
dwarf tellin, 103
dwarf-tellin, northern
Dyspanopeus sayi, 125
E
earthworms, marine, 55
Echinarachnius parma, 137
eel grass, 175
eel-grass, 175
eelgrass, common, 175
Elachista spp., 154
Elachistea spp., 154
Electra spp., 59
Emerita talpoida, 120
Ensis directus, 102
Enteromorpha
    intestinalis, 149
    linza, 150
Epitonium
    lineatum, 69
    rupicola, 69
Eubranchus
    exiguus, 86
    pallidus, 86
Eupleura caudate, 76
Euspira
    heros, 73
    triseriata, 74
F
fiddler,
    Atlantic marsh, 127
    Atlantic sand, 127
    calico-backed, 127
    mud, 127
    redjointed, 127
    sand, 127
filaments,
    green beaded, 150
    green tangled, 150
Flabellina
    gracilis, 86
    salmonacea, 86

verrucosa, 87
flatworm, speckled, 44
Flustra foliacea, 58
Fox Harbour Provincial Park, NS, 183
fringe, tufted, 154
Frond-aeolis, 85
Fucus
    distichous, 161
    distichus, 161
    evanescens, 161
    serratus, 161
    spiralis, 161
    vesiculosus, 160
Fundy National Park, NB, 189
G
Gammarus oceanicus, 117
gaper,
    blunt, 107
    mud, 107
Geukensia demissa, 93
Gigartina
    cornopifolia, 170
    stellata, 170
glasswort, 175
glassy bubble, solitary, 81
Glycera dibranchiate, 49
goat tang, 165
goose-tongue, 176
green algae, hollow, 149
green cord seaweed, 150
green fleece, 151
green laver, 149
Green Point, NB, 187
green weed, hollow, 149
gribble, 115
    northern, 115
grubby, 145
gunnel, rock, 146
H
Halibut Point State Park, MA, 197
Halichondria
    bowerbanki, 29
    panacea, 29
Haliclona
    oculata, 28
    permollis, 28
Haliplanella
    lineate, 31
    luciae, 31
Halosaccion ramentaceum, 168
Haminoea solitaria, 81
hard clam, 105
Harding Beach, Cape Cod, MA, 198
Harmothoe
    extenuata, 48